Protecting
Your Income
A N D
Your Family's
Future

Protecting Your Income
AND
Your Family's Future

Wm. Brock Thoene

BETHANY HOUSE PUBLISHERS
MINNEAPOLIS, MINNESOTA 55438
A Division of Bethany Fellowship, Inc.

Published by Bethany House Publishers
A Division of Bethany Fellowship, Inc.
6820 Auto Club Road, Minneapolis, Minnesota 55438

Printed in the United States of America

Library of Congress Cataloging-in-Publication Data

Thoene, Wm. Brock, 1952–
    Protecting your income and your family's future / Wm. Brock Thoene.
        p. cm.

    1. Finance, Personal. 2. Finance, Personal—Religious aspects—Christianity.
I. Title.
HG179.T455   1989
332.024—dc19   88–32753
ISBN 1-55661-044-0   CIP

Even though she will be reluctant to accept the credit, it is nevertheless true that this book would not and could not have happened without the loving, prayerful support of my greatest blessing: my wife, Bodie.

Therefore, it's to her this work is affectionately dedicated.

WM. BROCK THOENE (Tānē) is the manager of one of the largest Prudential Insurance Agencies in Central California. Since receiving a B.A. from Baylor University and an M.A. in Education from Cal State University, he has been in financial planning for ten years. During that time he has assisted hundreds of families in successfully structuring their financial future. He and his wife, Bodie, also work together as a writing team on both historical fiction and non-fiction projects. They make a home for their four children on a ranch in California.

Acknowledgments

The author would like to recognize the assistance provided by Marlene Meservey.

She was not only faithful to type, but even better, she was quick to encourage! My thanks.

There were also many other folks whose valuable suggestions and timely help made this work possible. To all of them, I offer my appreciation, as well.

Table of Contents

Introduction 11

PART I—PREPARING FOR FINANCIAL MANAGEMENT

1. Poverty 19
2. Proper Attitudes Toward Finances................. 31
3. Tithing, Budgets and Credit...................... 43

PART II—RISK MANAGEMENT

4. What the Bible Says About Insurance 61
5. Automobile Insurance............................. 67
6. Homeowner Insurance 85
7. Health Insurance................................. 101
8. Disability Insurance 111
9. Life Insurance Policies........................... 129
10. Life Insurance: How Much Is Enough? 147

PART III—INVESTMENT MANAGEMENT

11. Investment Basics................................ 165
12. Investment Choices 173
13. Retirement Planning 193

APPENDICES

Appendix A—Social Security.......................... 207
Appendix B—Choosing Advisors 211
Appendix C—The Importance of a Will................ 217

A CHRISTIAN FINANCIAL CREED 221

Introduction

JASON AND CELIA AUSTIN were newlyweds—at least they still thought of themselves that way—they had been married only eighteen months.

Jason had been working his way up in the supermarket, having recently been appointed assistant manager of the produce department. Celia was also working outside the home since they had no children as yet. Together they were trying to set aside enough cash to make a down payment on a home. Their living expenses were modest so far, and even though their combined income was less than $1800 a month, Jason and Celia were able to save approximately $400 each month.

Jason, being a good citizen, realized that the state in which he and Celia reside requires that he carry public liability and property damage protection on their automobile. Though young and in a high-rate category, Jason and Celia elected to save part of the premium cost by opting for minimum coverage.

After dropping Jason off at work one day, Celia was leaving the supermarket parking lot when, because of a moment's inattention, disaster struck. Celia failed to notice a two-year-old toddler who ran away from her mother and directly into the path of Celia's car. The child was killed instantly.

The child's parents, while well aware of how distraught and truly sorry Celia was, succumbed to a local attorney's TV ads promising to get them all they had coming.

Knowing that a sympathetic jury would undoubtedly consent to the half-million dollar settlement being sought, Jason and Celia's attorney agreed to an out-of-court settlement for $200,000. Jason and Celia's insurance company paid the "policy limits"—a cash sum of $25,000—to the child's parents. That left a $175,000 debt to be satisfied out of Jason's and Celia's weekly paychecks for the foreseeable future. They will spend all their savings and a great portion of their future earnings to satisfy this obligation.

Jim and Nora Branch are a retired couple living on a combination of Jim's pension, Social Security and some small assistance from their grown children. Their combined income is approximately $1200 a month. From this amount they are paying $400 in rent, approximately $200 a month for groceries, $100 a month for utilities and $100 a month for car expenses and other miscellaneous costs. The remainder of their monthly income is taken up one way or another by Jim's medical bills, which (although he receives Medicare payments as does Nora) eat up their remaining income. Jim and Nora's children are concerned and anxious to help, but are in the child-rearing years themselves and don't have a lot of extra capital.

Jim and Nora are holding the line financially, but they worry constantly about what will happen to them if either one hits a major medical crisis, or if their rent is raised significantly, or if the cost of food continues to increase, or if their car breaks down. Nora says, "We could live another twenty years!" She is not rejoicing in this fact.

Bill and Betty Seymour are a couple in the prime of life. Bill has had an enterprising career since college as an engineer. He and Betty have raised two children to college age and they still have two more living at home. They have had no difficulties in supporting a $1000-a-month mortgage payment and their grocery and incidental bills, which run around $800 a month. Bill has even been able to put aside money in an IRA with which he anticipates a comfortable retirement. Bill has often described himself as "insurance poor," since he pays for automobile insurance on five cars, his homeowner insurance, the dependent portion of the cost of his company's medical insurance and several long-standing life insurance plans.

Today, however, Bill is not thinking about how much he has paid in insurance premiums; he is dismally regarding the news from his doctor that the back pains he's been experiencing are an advancing and degenerative form of arthritis. Bill realizes that his ability to work at a drafting table is about to end. His doctor has been able to alleviate the symptoms somewhat through medication, but the pain killers make Bill drowsy and are as much responsible for the decline in his ability to work as is the disease. Bill believes he will soon be placed on a disability leave from his company. The company benefits will continue to pay his salary in full for six months, after which Bill and Betty wonder what they will do.

What happened to all these families? Did they plan to fail? No, rather they failed to plan. Let's look now at some families that have done adequate planning. For these folks the outcome of similar life situations would be far different from those we have just seen.

Take Mike and Ruth Haley, a retired couple. Early on in their working years Mike and Ruth regularly set aside a percentage of their income toward retirement savings. Though painful at times, they followed the advice, "Pay yourself first." Right after the tithe to their local church, they did just that.

Mike and Ruth never changed the percentage of income they saved each month. But their income-producing ability increased, and so did the size of their nest egg. As tax-saver programs became available, such as IRA's, Mike and Ruth contributed to these also. As their savings grew, they began to attend financial planning seminars and to seek professional advice on how best to invest for safety and growth potential.

Now, as both are approaching the age of seventy, Mike and Ruth have converted all of their savings into tax-free municipal bond trust units paying them a completely tax-free income both guaranteed and insured in the amount of $4000 per month. Mike and Ruth love doing things for their children, grandchildren and their newborn great-grandchild.

Allen and Jan Barnes were devastated when a tree in their backyard, weakened by a rainstorm, dropped a large branch, killing a neighbor's child. Allen and Jan believe that their life will eventually get back to normal, but right now they are grateful to God for the forethought that allowed them to purchase a one million-dollar umbrella liability policy. Far from losing their home and other assets in a court battle, their insurance offered them the level of protection they never expected to need.

Finally, let's look at Bill and Nancy Flynn. Bill was a rising young real estate agent, his wife a beautiful and devoted mother of twins. Bill had never had a sick day in his life it seemed—never been hospitalized, never had a broken bone. They had recently purchased a larger home, one that would give them more room for their children's growth years.

Then Bill was discovered to have pancreatic cancer. In spite of the best medical care available, Bill died in less than six months.

When they purchased their new home, Bill and Nancy opted to increase their life insurance protection, taking out an additional $100,000 policy on each of them. This amount was paid to Nancy within ten days of Bill's death. It completely paid off the mortgage and their remaining debts, including two car payments. Bill had also taken out a $150,000 policy at the time he married Nancy, and this sum—since it was a universal life policy with an increasing death benefit—now paid Nancy $180,000.

Following some diligent and prayerful counseling, Nancy has opted to invest the $180,000 in a balanced mutual fund, consisting of a mixture of blue chip stocks and bonds. Nancy expects to receive about $18,000 a year in earnings from the investment. While this amount will not sustain her for the rest of her life, nor put the twins through college, Nancy feels that the $1500 a month it represents will be enough for her and the children to live on (they are, at this point, debt free) while she goes back to school to complete her teaching credentials.

Nancy will always miss Bill, but she will be forever thankful that he thought enough of her to do some serious life insurance planning.

In reviewing any set of examples, there is a tendency to adopt an "it-could-never-happen-to-me" stance. This is particularly true where the case histories involve tragic or dramatic circumstances. A reminder: the folks whose anecdotes were just recounted felt that their own situations were unremarkable *right up until the moment* when an unforseen occurrence altered their futures. For every example given, there are literally thousands of people who *could* say "that almost happened to me" and even more families who *should* think "that might have been us."

There is a very clear difference between the first set of examples and the ones you've just read. There seems to be a fairly simple answer as to why this is so. All the families in the first examples planned inadequately. They based their futures on inaccurate or incomplete advice. They failed to take a longer view. They failed to consider real, possible hazards to their income and family security.

It is my prayer that this book will enable you—and those loved ones for whom you are responsible—to become financially secure and protected, and to apply godly principles to your family financial planning—beginning with this admonition:

> Be very careful, then, how you live—not as unwise but as wise, making the most of every opportunity, because the days are evil. Therefore do not be foolish, but understand what the Lord's will is. (Eph. 5:15–17)

PART ONE

Preparing for Financial Management

1

Poverty

It WAS FRIDAY night, the end of a grueling week of mid-term exams. My new wife, Bodie, and I breathed sighs of relief and decided to celebrate by splurging on a bucket of chicken and a drive-in movie. We popped our own popcorn (without butter—it cost too much), and we brought our own iced tea.

Spreading a blanket on the hood of our old car, we sat beneath the stars and watched *Fiddler on the Roof*. We could not have enjoyed ourselves more. Never mind that the wiper blades dug into our backs and mosquitos hummed in our ears; we laughed heartily as the milkman, Tevye, sang to God and the squawking chickens in his barnyard. He asked if it would spoil the divine plan if God were to make him a wealthy man.

As we watched Tevye discuss his own poverty with the Lord, it didn't penetrate our contented minds that we had spent our last dollar getting into the movie. Tevye was better off than we were! At least he owned his milk cows and chickens. We, on the other hand, were living in student housing and struggling to stretch a budget that put us well below what was at the time "poverty level." Fortunately, we were too carefree and happy to know we should have been *worried* and *unhappy*. We had signed up "for richer or poorer," and even in this poorer stage we were having fun.

The years brought children, bills and a mortgage and, like it or not, we came face-to-face with the reality that poverty was no longer an adventure. Being broke is not fun.

The Bible has a great deal to say about the reality of poverty, since it is a problem that has plagued the earth from the beginning of time. Jesus recognized the problem of poverty and once commented, "The poor you have with you always." Two thousand years have not changed the situation and, inasmuch as poverty is the opposite of being "well off," let's see where you stand in your balancing act with finances.

Are you rich and hoping to avoid poverty?

Are you barely scraping by and trying not to slip into financial disaster?

Are you poor and simply wishing that you could make ends meet?

Whatever category you fit into, there are five scriptural principles regarding finances that you must know.

Principle #1:
God's Ownership of All Finances and Belongings

The first principle is this: God is the owner and distributor of money and material possessions. Hannah, the mother of the prophet Samuel, addressed this issue in a portion of her prayer at Samuel's dedication to the Lord:

> The Lord brings death and makes alive; he brings down to the grave and raises up. The Lord sends poverty and wealth; he humbles and he exalts. He raises the poor from the dust and lifts the needy from the ash heap; he seats them with princes and has them inherit a throne of honor. For the foundations of the earth are the Lord's; upon them he has set the world. (1 Sam. 2:6–8)

Until we get a handle on the fact that "the Lord sends poverty and wealth," until we cease clinging to our possessions, until we abandon any idea that security in this life comes through investments, we will not be able to fully enjoy the earthly blessings over which God has given us temporary stewardship.

The most contented and successful businessmen of my acquaintance are those who say sincerely: "God owns my business." Each of them acknowledges a responsibility to be as good an employee as possible for God, while relishing the freedom found in being able to say to God, "I don't know why you've chosen to allow such a circumstance to exist or what your thinking is in causing such an unexpected event at this time—but whatever you think, after all, this is your business!"

What these men and women have learned is an attitude of trust—the belief that God knows what's best for us, His children. Putting our entire lives into His hands (yes, even our bankbooks and our mortgage payments!) will not result in some kind of catastrophe as a sadistic puppet master "tests" our faithfulness.

I must quickly point out that there is no time when one has "arrived" at complete trust. In my work, I counsel young couples on how to stretch $1000 to cover a month's worth of food, housing, transportation and insurance. Do they need more or less trust than the middle-aged professional whose monthly income need is $6000 and for whom a 3-month illness would mean the loss of both present and future income?

Have you thanked God for your home? When you go to the grocery store, are you consciously grateful that you can pay for your family's needs? Have you asked God to bless your automobile with safety of operation? Have you offered to use it as He directs? Do you feel that tithing is giving God something of yours—or do you see it as returning to Him a fraction of what is already His?

Alone, or as a couple, take out a sheet of paper and begin making a list. What are the possessions God has given you— your home, your car, your income? What things are you most frightened of losing—your job, your savings, your standard of living? What financial plans are of greatest concern to you—your children's education, owning your own business, retiring comfortably?

This project may get completed in an evening or it may be that you will start the list and add to it as God brings things to your mind over a period of several days. When it feels complete, when you are satisfied that it is exhaustive, take it and your paycheck and lay them both on the altar of God's ownership.

You might want to pray a prayer something like this:

> Heavenly Father, as I hold my paycheck and a list of concerns in my hand, may I be reminded that it is a gift from you, as are all my physical possessions. Help me to consciously dedicate them all to your service. Help me to show myself to be a good "employee" of yours, putting the things you have blessed me with to good use and management. At the same time, help me to trust you completely and to relax in your ownership and planning. Amen.

Principle #2:

God Has Concern for the Poor

God has a *particular* concern for protecting the rights of the poor. That is because they often are without any other benefactor. Solomon says:

> Do not exploit the poor because they are poor and do not crush the needy in court, for the Lord will take up their case and will plunder those who plunder them. (Prov. 22:22–23)

Before David was king of Israel, he spent some time on the run from King Saul. David was forced to live away from comfortable surroundings, even hiding in a cave and forced for a time to be dependent on the generosity of others for his subsistence. By anyone's standards he was poor. Consequently it was out of personal experience that he was able to write:

> I know that the Lord secures justice for the poor and upholds the cause of the needy. (Ps. 140:12)

Because God takes special interest in the poor, we must

be very careful in our attitude toward poverty, or lack. Now you may be thinking, "Wait a minute, everyone's against poverty." True, we are against the concept and we are certainly against being poor. But do we view the poor of the world through God's eyes—with compassion and interest for their well-being? Or are we happier thinking that there is a government agency or charitable organization responsible for them?

Webster's Ninth New Collegiate Dictionary defines poverty as:

The state of one who lacks a usual or *socially acceptable* amount of money or material possessions (emphasis mine).

Not only are we instructed *not* to exploit or mistreat the poor, as Isaiah says:

Woe to those who make unjust laws, to those who issue oppressive decrees, to deprive the poor of their rights and rob my oppressed people of justice, making widows their prey and robbing the fatherless. (Isa. 10:1–2)

We are further urged to not even show favoritism for a rich person over a poor one. James says:

Listen, my dear brothers: Has not God chosen those who are poor in the eyes of the world to be rich in faith and to inherit the kingdom he promised those who love him? (James 2:5)

Michael Harrington, in his work *The Other America*, wrote:

People who are much too sensitive to demand of cripples that they run races ask of the poor that they get up and act just like everyone else in the society.

Prayerfully read and ponder James 2. Do you understand that God has a special love for those who cannot properly feed and clothe themselves? Is there anything in your attitude or actions toward the poor that God is asking you to change?

Heavenly Father, help me to see the poor, and all who are less fortunate than I, through your eyes of compassion and love. Help me to truly keep the "royal law" of loving my neighbor as myself, without any hint of favoritism. Help me to stand up for and speak out for those who cannot do so for themselves. Amen.

Principle #3:

We Have Certain Responsibilities Toward the Poor

I will never forget Mrs. Nichols, a large woman with very black skin, warm brown eyes and glistening white teeth that flashed behind her constant smile. When I was a boy, she worked as a housekeeper for several families in our neighborhood. Every day she arrived on the bus, carrying a satchel over her arm. She knew every kid in the neighborhood by name and spoke to us as we walked to school.

I remember that her dress was always clean and pressed, and yet it was always one of two—either the black dress or the brown one. Her shoes were rundown at the heels and her big feet seemed ready to break out of the leather. She had six children at home to support on the meager wages of a housekeeper. Mrs. Nichols was what we called a "poor" woman. Still, she smiled and called out to us by name.

In the afternoon on my way home from school, I would often hear her voice drifting from the window of the house where she worked . . . "Just a closer walk with thee. Grant it Jesus, if you please. Daily walking close to thee—Let it be, dear Lord, let it be!"

Mrs. Nichols, from the poor side of town, was a neighborhood landmark. She could scold you or offer you cookies; she knew a lot about kids. And not a white kid in that whole middle-class neighborhood grew up during those years without hearing about the love of Jesus.

As poor as Mrs. Nichols was, I now understand that she knew there were those with greater needs than her own. First, she evidently saw the poverty of souls who had never known physical hunger or want. That was us . . . the kids in my neighborhood . . . the place where Santa stopped whether or not we deserved it. Mrs. Nichols was a sort of missionary who arrived every morning on the bus, loaded down with songs and good words.

Eventually, she began to tell us about the kids who lived in her neighborhood. This was a place Santa usually forgot even when the kids deserved a visit. Some families were hungry, abandoned and without hope or help. Mrs. Nichols became their ambassador and we spread out like an army of determined midgets to round up canned food and clothes we had outgrown. Our mothers caught the spirit of the thing and drove carloads of stuff to Mrs. Nichols' church at regular intervals throughout the coming years.

From those experiences, the poverty of our souls found nourishment. New friendships were formed and lives changed on both sides of the track. You see, Mrs. Nichols knew you don't have to be rich in order to fulfill your responsibilities to the poor.

God extends His concern for the poor by making it our responsibility to assist them. Just as soon as the Hebrews left the slave conditions of Egypt and became more well-to-do, they were admonished:

> If there is a poor man among your brothers in any of the towns of the land that the Lord your God is giving you, do not be hardhearted or tightfisted toward your poor brother. Rather be openhanded and freely lend him whatever he needs. (Deut. 15:7–8)

This commandment also contains the proper attitude we must assume in giving, and it includes a promise:

> Give generously to him and do so without a grudging heart; then because of this the Lord your God will bless you in all your work and in everything you put your hand to. (Deut. 15:10)

Whom do you know personally who is in financial difficulty? Is the Lord bringing to mind right now a family whose provider has been laid off from work? Is there an older couple you know who would be blessed if you could assist them?

We need not always think of giving to the poor as providing money. Are you in a position to offer a job to someone who needs employment? Could you lend a car to a family without transportation? How about offering a ride to work to someone unable to return the favor? Are you willing to commit yourself to taking one meal a week to a single-parent household? Do you know how the benevolence committee at your church works? How much of the church offering goes to help the needy in your community? If you met a needy family, would you know how your congregation would be able to assist them?

> Heavenly Father, as I view the food in my cupboard and the clothes in my closet, bring to my mind those whom you would have me assist. Help me to be conscious of their needs and sensitive to their feelings. Correct in me any thoughts that are not generous and loving. Make me a practical expression of your concern for their lives. Amen.

Principle #4:
God Uses Poverty to Teach Us Two Valuable Lessons

Mrs. Nichols did much more than just arrange a sharing of food and clothing among the needy in our city. She made those of us who were able to help sense our responsibility: We felt like God's agents and we enjoyed the feeling. (She called us *angels*, a phrase no one else applied to us kids!) She also helped us sense God's provision for His children. As we saw families being blessed, we caught a glimpse of heavenly concern for practical matters—a view of the "gospel in shoe leather" that we would never have found through Bible school alone.

What are the two lessons God wants to teach us? First, God uses times of financial distress to bring us to a more complete trust and reliance on Him. Proverbs says:

> Whoever trusts in his riches will fall, but the righteous will thrive like a green leaf. (Prov. 11:28)

How is it with you? Do you think you can work your way out of debt, but keep the same attitudes that brought you there? Do you think you have enough savings to weather any financial storm? Will your "suitable investments" and "adequate insurance" completely insulate you against disaster? Are you trusting God—or trusting in financial planning?

These sorts of questions would seem to argue against the need for or the validity of a book such as the one you are now holding. But remember Principle #1: If you are acting as God's employee, His "steward," He wants you to be an effective money manager. But first (and forever after) you must recognize your complete reliance on Him.

The second lesson God expects us to learn from poverty is this: We have a divine commission to act as God's channel of blessing to those less fortunate than ourselves. Like Mrs. Nichols, we need to remember that there is not a magic line we cross from being unable to help to being providers. There are any number of nonmonetary, creative, Holy-Spirit-inspired ways to assist others.

The Apostle Paul wrote this about the Macedonian churches:

> We want you to know about the grace that God has given the Macedonian churches. Out of the most severe trial, their overflowing joy and their extreme poverty welled up in rich generosity. For I testify that they gave as much as they were able, and even beyond their ability. (2 Cor. 8:1)

Learn to see your responsibility as God's instrument of blessing in a new light. Can you see that with increased wealth and property come increases in responsibility? Who is the Holy Spirit bringing to your mind right now? What needs do they have?

> Heavenly Father, let me pay attention to the twin lessons of poverty. First, help me to keep my trust in you alone. May I never be guilty of relying on money or property. Second, make me ever conscious of those whose needs you would use me to meet. May others be able to praise your name because I listened to your leading. Amen.

Principle #5:
God's Word Gives Warnings to Help Us Avoid Poverty

While God's Word acknowledges that poverty *will* exist, He has made us thinking rational beings capable of good (and bad) money management decisions. Accordingly, He has given us a set of warnings against the causes of poverty. There are numerous references throughout the book of Proverbs to the things that cause lack, and they can be grouped into five categories: laziness, ostentatious display, poor planning, greed and dishonesty.

Laziness

Laziness means a lack of discipline, or sloth.

> Lazy hands make a man poor, but diligent hands bring wealth. (Prov. 10:4)

> He who ignores discipline comes to poverty and shame, but whoever heeds correction is honored. (Prov. 13:18)

These passages obviously refer to working your hardest, but they also relate to diligent studying and application of sound money management principles.

Ostentatious Display

Proverbs also warns us to guard against overindulging in whims, or in an excessive display of wealth. Some people who love money are not misers in the classic sense—loving money for its own sake—but they desire more and more money to "keep up appearances." Yet:

> He who loves pleasure will become poor; whoever loves wine and oil will never be rich. (Prov. 21:17)

This does not mean we shouldn't enjoy the good things of life that God gives us, or feel guilty if God permits us to live comfortably. It *does* mean that we are to focus on God and be grateful for what He has provided, rather than focusing on the "things" we enjoy.

Poor Planning

Proverbs tells us that ill-considered plans or "get-rich-quick" schemes lead to poverty.

> The plans of the diligent lead to profit as surely as haste

leads to poverty. (Prov. 21:5)

Another verse adds:

All hard work brings a profit, but mere talk leads only to poverty. (Prov. 14:23)

Don't expect to find in this book (or anywhere else, for that matter) a magic formula for financial success. God's Word will point us in the right direction only through dedicated research and use.

Greed

Greed is reproved in Scripture. Someone who amasses money for its own sake or gathers possessions in excess of his need and comfort is told to expect poverty.

A stingy man is eager to get rich and is unaware that poverty awaits him. (Prov. 28:22)

It is worth noting that you don't have to be rich to be greedy.

Dishonesty

Wealth gained through dishonest actions (stealing, bribery) or dishonest talk (lies, flattery) is part of a downward spiral into poverty.

The Lord abhors dishonest scales, but accurate weights are his delight. (Prov. 11:1)

Prov. 22:16 adds:

He who oppresses the poor to increase his wealth and he who gives gifts to the rich—both come to poverty.

God cares more about the condition of your heart than the condition of your pocketbook (although He cares about that, too). And an impoverished spirit is more destructive than an impoverished bank account.

Where is your attitude about finances in light of the advice given in Proverbs? Do you struggle with laziness? Are you tempted to flaunt a new car . . . does it irk you to drive a car that isn't stylish or brand new? Are you guilty of chasing schemes for instant wealth? Does your life show the evidence of greed? Would you turn a blind eye toward dishonest business practices at your work place?

> Heavenly Father, thank you for giving me instruction in how to avoid poverty. Let my work and study be disciplined; let me enjoy your blessings without flaunting them or continually chasing after more. Grant that I may be as wise in planning as I am empty of greed. Keep me from dishonesty of thought, word or deed. Amen.

Concluding Thoughts

You see, the opposite of poverty is not wealth, but having enough to meet your needs. God has not promised to endow us with excessive money or belongings but to fulfill our requirements. We need to remember that the good things we enjoy are to remind us of God's blessing and beyond that to share the blessing with others.

Reviewing My Personal Situation:
What the Bible Says About Poverty

1. True or False: Wealth can be obtained through hard work.
2. True or False: Wealth automatically makes one a sinner.
3. True or False: I take pride in my work and work diligently at my job.
4. True or False: I buy things I don't really need and indulge in frivolous purchases.
5. True or False: I am attracted to get-rich-quick schemes.
6. True or False: I have trouble parting with even one dollar I've earned.
7. True or False: I think "shading the truth" on my tax return is okay.

2

Proper Attitudes Toward Finances

THE PARABLE of the talents in Matthew 25 tells of a propertied man who knows something about investment. When he must set out on a long journey, he calls in three servants and divides the management and supervision of his assets among them. The first servant is given responsibility for 5 talents—let's say that's $5000. The second, 2 talents, and the third, 1.

In the master's absence the first two servants succeed in doubling the owner's money. The third servant, however, "dug a hole in the ground and hid his master's money."

When the master returns, he interviews each servant to settle accounts. Upon hearing the good news from each of the first two servants, he not only rewards them, but places them in charge of future endeavors. The third servant is a completely different story.

Immediately, the servant excuses his poor management, saying:

Master . . . I knew that you are a hard man. . . . So I was afraid and went out and hid your talent in the ground. See, here is what belongs to you. [Note the criticism directed at his master.]

Swiftly, the master replies:

You wicked, lazy servant! . . . You should have put my money on deposit with the bankers, so that when I returned I would have received it back with interest. . . . Take the talent from him and give it to the one who has ten talents. . . . And throw that worthless servant outside, into the darkness, where there will be weeping and gnashing of teeth.

This parable instructs us in the proper use of our God-given callings and abilities. But taken at face value, it also conveys that it is correct and appropriate to be a good money manager. If we take the attitude that all our possessions and income are really being held in trust for the Lord, then the financial application of this parable is more clear.

It's interesting to note the heavy criticism of the servant who kept the Lord's wealth safe, but who showed no increase because it meant taking some risk to do so. Very few people are endowed with an innate sense of wise investment techniques. Consequently, making proper and productive use of finances requires education and diligent consideration for most of us.

The Scriptural Basis for Financial Management

Let's reexamine Paul's statement to the Ephesians:

Be very careful, then, how you live—not as unwise but as wise, making the most of every opportunity, because the days are evil. Therefore do not be foolish, but understand what the Lord's will is. (Eph. 5:15–17)

He is clearly advising us in regard to our spiritual walk—but his words can also be applied to the whole of life. If we believe that our financial health is of interest to God and that our monetary decisions must line up with His will, we have to face some facts. Primarily, it's impossible to "make the most of every opportunity" without examining the risks involved in financial decisions. When we understand the threats to our financial health, we then (1) search for the means to avoid those hazards and (2) take steps to implement the correct solutions. As with any other aspect of life, it is not possible to pray intelligently or make correct choices in regard to finances without a basic understanding. From study and prayer, a plan that is right for you will emerge.

Two Extreme Positions

During my years in financial management, I have encountered two extremes of believers. Folks at one extreme believe God does *not* want them to have any concern for their lives or material possessions. They believe that buying insurance is offensive to God—that its purchase runs counter to completely relying on the Lord's protection.

Early in my career I encountered a young couple who held this point of view. That is to say, the husband did. He purchased the absolute minimum in auto liability coverage (and only because a state law required it). He absolutely refused to consider any life insurance. During one interview he was called away to the phone. Then his wife confided that, because of their three young children, she had urged him to reconsider but he refused. He maintained that buying life insurance betrayed a lack of faith in God's protection. Since these are his firmly held convictions (and because he is still living as of this writing), I cannot dispute his conclusions— *in his case*. I have seen ample evidence in other families, however, that life insurance can be a real blessing from God and definitely part of His plan. (The spiritual basis for insurance is discussed on page 38ff., and in chapter four.)

The second extreme "spiritual" position is, ironically, to leave out the Lord altogether. There are those who believe that money decisions are too mundane or "unspiritual" to be of any interest to the Lord. These folks have adopted the attitude that God expects us to muddle through on our own and not bother Him with questions about investments or budgets. Consequently, they have only worldly wisdom to consult in this important matter.

The vast majority, though, fall somewhere in a great middle ground. They feel inadequate to maximize their family's financial potential. They do not have even basic information on the subject, and so they cannot even pray intelligently for assistance. Nor do they know where to get the needed information.

Which of the three groups pictured above do you fit into?

Christians, like everyone else, have problems managing their money. Like others, we feel that professional advice in financial matters is too costly, or that our concerns are too trivial to interest a "high-powered professional." We suspect that a financial expert has motives of self-interest; that he or she only wants to sell us something. In short, we don't ask for vital help when it comes to money.

This book is intended to help folks at any stage of financial development. Are you a young person just beginning a career? Are you part of a family struggling to maintain credit-card debts? Have you been successful in saving some money but aren't sure if it's correctly invested? Whatever your monetary picture, I'd like to help you develop a clear-cut picture of some basic financial truths, offered within the general framework of God's Word and God's will for your life.

Understanding Financial Management

The phrase "financial planning" has come to be bandied about by so many professionals, amateurs, and media people that it is almost without content or meaning. An attorney, a CPA, an insurance agent, or a self-styled "financial planner" would each put a different spin on the ball, giving you a view that might not be of maximum benefit to you and your situation.

With so many opinions to review, let's try to put limits on our definition by explaining what financial management is *not* before setting down what it *is*.

What Financial Management Is Not

First of all, financial management is not a "get-rich-quick" scheme; no plan can guarantee vast wealth. It does not imply a reliance on a particular economic philosophy, stock market strategy, investment method or choice of product. While proper financial management will emphasize some common sense rules of investment and savings, no endorsement of a particular institution or profession is implied by the phrase.

Many people have accepted a slanted definition from the source who first gave them advice: "financial planning," through the banker's eyes, may mean purchasing certificates of deposit. An insurance agent's perspective may mean purchasing more insurance. A stockbroker may advise a systematic investment in utility stocks. While all of these counselors are necessary in various portions of financial management— and all of their products have appropriate places in a family's long-term plan—each of these explanations is too narrow. None of them constitute the financial strategy itself.

Without a Clear Definition, How Successful Are Most People at Financial Management?

Financial management has a broad definition. It needs to include the structure of a family's financial future, both short- and long-term. It should include elements of proper insurance planning, investment choices, tax strategy and estate planning. All of these diverse areas must meld into a comprehensive outline to which specific choices are added. Each time a short-term goal is reached, the program must be reevaluated and needed adjustments made.

Does this sound like a process requiring study and constant review? It is. And the lack of proper thought prior to monetary decisions may permanently stunt the investment's ability to grow; failing to reexamine and adjust can cause a financial plan to bottom out.

Information published by the U.S. Department of Health and Human Services reveals that out of 100 people who begin their working lifetime at age 25, only 3 have annual incomes of $25,000 or more upon retirement at age 65. With 40 years in which to plan and 40 years worth of income, 68 of those good folks have failed in some measure to reach the goal of retiring comfortably. (See chart on p. 204.)

This sad fact can be attributed to a number of different causes: financial reversals, catastrophic health problems, the state of the national economy, improper advice or simply the failure to start soon enough. But mostly it's a result of the fact that most of those sixty-eight people simply failed to do their homework. To borrow a cliche (which has a definite ring of truth!), "They didn't plan to fail; they failed to plan."

Financial Management Defined

So what *is* financial management?

Financial management must concern itself with two broad areas of a family's economic health. The first is *risk management*. This means taking stock of those things that would disrupt the flow of spendable income and, where possible, reducing the hazard. For instance, driving an automobile without adequate liability insurance is a hazard to a family's economic well-being that needs to be corrected. Another example is lacking an understanding of how your family would be affected by a long-term illness or a disability. Such a review may involve nothing more than some time spent in studying your employer's provisions for this sort of emergency; unpleasant surprises due to misunderstood protection can be devastating. Financial planning may not always involve purchasing stocks, bonds or a new policy, but it *will* always involve study and thoughtful consideration.

The second broad area of financial management is the wise handling of investments. If the word "investment" sounds more grandiose in light of the present condition of your checkbook, think of the word "savings" instead. Either way, this part of financial management means deciding where to put that part of your income which is to be used for future needs. Preparing for your children's education belongs in this category as does preparing for your retirement. The issues involved here are the safety of your money, its availability when needed, and how much of it will be left for your use after taxes.

The Four Steps in Financial Management

The first step in a financial strategy is quite simple. Review each area of your family's economic program with two questions in mind: What is the situation now and what do I want the situation to be? In other words, what aspect of your present plan can be improved?

> EXAMPLE: Barry and Gail Barnum are discussing retirement. Barry has no retirement plan through his employment, and they have read with concern some articles about the projected inadequacy of Social Security. The Barnums' savings never seem to build up past a certain point because it gains interest so slowly and is too easily accessible.

Second, before making a decision on how to change their present financial structure, Barry and Gail have to study a list of appropriate options.

> Barry proposes that they increase the size of their monthly savings deposit. Gail has heard that they can purchase U.S. Savings Bonds through Barry's work, and feels that they would be less likely to spend their savings if it were in that form. The Barnums' insurance agent also makes a presentation about Individual Retirement Accounts. They begin to consider these options.

Third, there comes a point when all the information has been gathered and the facts weighed and considered and it's time to make a decision. This part is called *implementation.*

> The Barnums conclude that the tax advantages of the IRA make it an ideal choice for their situation. Barry signs an annuity contract with their insurance company to deposit $100 per month toward retirement.

The fourth and final step in successful financial management is reviewing and adjusting. No decision is permanent or even always adequate. As a family's situation changes, as needs change, previous decisions must be subjected again to steps one through three. We can think of this as *correcting the course.*

> At the first annual review of the IRA, the Barnums are dis-

appointed with the annuity's current interest figure. They assemble an alternative list of IRA investments including banks and mutual funds and elect to make no further contributions to the annuity but begin sending their $100 per month to a mutual fund company instead.

It is always appropriate to ask for advice. You may only wish for help in understanding the various choices as presented by their proponents, or you may want to seek assistance in other parts of the process as well. Sometimes it's helpful to have an outsider* assist with the initial review since our pocketbooks and our emotions may be too closely tied together to feel comfortable in decision-making. Remember also that a *review* does not necessarily require a purchase or a change in your present plan. Be aware, however, that not making a change when one is required is the *worst* kind of decision possible.

Beginning the Planning Process With the Proper Attitudes

Often the only thing distinguishing a Christian's financial planning from that which is practiced by the world is the matter of motivation. We are confronted with the same monetary dilemmas, after all, and must select from the same list of alternatives as everyone else.

Attitude # 1: Money Is Neither Good Nor Evil

It's important to realize that money and possessions are not, in themselves, either good or evil. They are inanimate objects incapable of causing anything either positive or negative to happen. First Tim. 6:10, which is frequently misquoted as saying "money is the root of all evil," actually reads:

For the *love* of money is a root of all kinds of evil.

Evil results from an *improper attitude toward money and not from the money itself.* As Eccles. 5:10 reports:

---

* See Appendix B.

Whoever loves money never has money enough; whoever loves wealth is never satisfied with his income.

The lack of money is no guarantee of spirituality either, as Prov. 30:7–9 records:

Two things I ask of you, O Lord; do not refuse me before I die: Keep falsehood and lies far from me; give me neither poverty nor riches, but give me only my daily bread. Otherwise, I may have too much and disown you and say, "Who is the Lord?" Or I may become poor and steal, and so dishonor the name of my God.

The way we regard our finances will inevitably lead in one of two directions: Either our attitude will lead us to an ever-increasing responsibility in God's kingdom as we evidence our faithfulness and stewardship, or our attitude toward wealth and possessions will pull us away from God. As Jesus warned:

Watch out! Be on your guard against all kinds of greed; a man's life does not consist in the abundance of his possessions. (Luke 12:15)

Attitude # 2: God Owns and Distributes All Possessions

As noted earlier, a believer must have firmly in mind a realization that God is the owner and the controller of all wealth and possessions *before* beginning financial management. Take note of the passage from Job 41:11 where God says:

Who has a claim against me that I must pay? Everything under heaven belongs to me.

This is so fundamental for a Christian that no other discussion of economic strategy will have true meaning without the prior recognition and acceptance of this principle. If you have trouble accepting this point of view, I want you to reflect on some factors still more basic. Did you choose your parents? Were you able to select the country of your birth or the year? Could you affect the financial condition into which you were born? Didn't God determine from before your birth what your beginning circumstances were going to be? Since you cannot guarantee your health, nor even draw one additional breath with absolute certainty, how can you take credit for (control of) the increase of your wealth or the additions to your possessions?

Attitude # 3: There Is No Security in Wealth

The immediate result of resigning your ownership of possessions to God's control is to become free from anxiety about them. Take note of Ezek. 7:19:

> Their silver and gold will not be able to save them in the day of the Lord's wrath. They will not satisfy their hunger or fill their stomachs with it, for it has made them stumble into sin.

There is no security in wealth, and only recognizing God's ownership of all that we temporarily possess frees us from worrying. As Jesus says in His great message on freedom from worry:

> Who of you by worrying can add a single hour to his life? . . . Do not worry, saying, "What shall we eat?" or "What shall we drink?" or "What shall we wear?" For the pagans run after all these things, and your heavenly Father knows that you need them. (Matt. 6:27, 31–32)

Then He adds this advice:

> Seek first his kingdom and his righteousness, and all these things will be given to you as well. (v. 33)

Attitude # 4: God Has Expectations of Our Stewardship

Does all this discussion of God's ownership mean that we should make no plans and take no steps in regard to material things? By no means. Throughout God's Word we see that He expects us—after we have acknowledged His ownership—to fulfill certain responsibilities.

First, we are expected to work hard. Prov. 28:19 says:

> He who works his land will have abundant food [or riches],

but the one who chases fantasies will have his fill of poverty.

Second, God expects us to deal fairly with all. Prov. 11:1 states:

> The Lord abhors dishonest scales, but accurate weights are his delight.

Third, we are obligated to return to God a part of what we have received. Prov. 3:9–10 issues a command and a promise:

> Honor the Lord with your wealth, with the firstfruits of all your crops; then your barns will be filled to overflowing, and your vats will brim over with new wine.

Finally—and it is from this point that a Christian properly embarks on a plan of financial management—God expects us to do our very best with what has been entrusted to our care. Prov. 6:6 reminds us:

> Go to the ant, you sluggard; consider its ways and be wise! It has no commander, no overseer or ruler, yet it stores its provisions in summer and gathers its food at harvest.

Review again the parable in Matthew 25, keeping in mind the two servants who were praised for successfully investing the Lord's provision.

Final Thoughts About Financial Management and Spiritual Attitudes

Financial well-being does not equate with spirituality any more than Job's tragedy meant that he had fallen out of favor with God. In all our subsequent discussions, we will be mindful that all good gifts come from our Father in heaven and we acknowledge His grace in allowing us to hold them for now. With this attitude it is possible to properly honor God by wisely managing those earthly blessings we've received.

God wants you to give back to His work out of the first of all you receive. Beyond that commitment He allows you to pay for your necessities and to enjoy a degree of comfort.

We are encouraged in Scripture to be wise money managers, to make adequate provision for emergencies, to be wise with investments so we do not become a burden to others and even to leave an inheritance for our children. As Prov. 13:22 says:

> A good man leaves an inheritance for his children's children, but a sinner's wealth is stored up for the righteous.

Prayerfully seek wisdom in regard to financial management. We want to take full advantage of the promise in Prov. 2:12:

> Wisdom will save you from the ways of wicked men, from men whose words are perverse.

And the one which follows it in Prov. 3:13–14:

> Blessed is the man who finds wisdom, the man who gains understanding, for she [Wisdom] is more profitable than silver and yields better returns than gold.

Reviewing My Personal Situation:

The Financial Management Process

1. Review the present situation: Where am I now and where do I want to be?
2. What are the possible decisions or choices appropriate to this situation?
3. Implementation: Make decisions when required.
4. Review and Adjust: Repeat steps 1, 2, and 3 regularly.

Remember: Seek advice as needed on any of the four steps.

3

Tithing, Budgets and Credit

WHAT MAKES a book about a Christian approach to financial planning different from a secular treatment of the same subject? After all, Christians need to purchase fire insurance just like anyone else and probably from the same sources. Banks don't look into your spirituality before offering to pay interest on your deposit, and a Christian's investments have no guarantee of success.

If the order of topics in the chapter title seems wrong, it's because priority is the first, discernible difference between the believer and nonbeliever. In God's economy, giving back to *Him* comes first.

Tithing

Isn't tithing a legalistic, Old Testament requirement that has no place among believers governed by grace? What is the scriptural basis for tithing?

In his excellent book, *Your Money Matters*, Malcolm MacGregor quotes Jesus as saying:

Woe to you, teachers of the law and Pharisees, you hypocrites! You give a tenth of your spices—mint, dill and cum-min. But you have neglected the more important matters of the law—justice, mercy and faithfulness. You should have practiced the latter, without neglecting the former. (Matt. 23:23)

MacGregor points out that Jesus was critical of the Phar-isees for not attending to justice, mercy and faithfulness, but He never questioned their faithfulness in tithing. In fact, Jesus specifically said they "should have practiced the latter" (justice, etc.), "without neglecting the former" (tithing).

So what is the first point in regard to tithing? It is *com-manded* by God. Lev. 27:30 says:

A tithe of everything from the land, whether grain from the soil or fruit from the trees, belongs to the lord; it is holy to the Lord.

The tithe amount is understood to be a tenth of your in-come. Its purpose is to support the activities of your local church, the salaries of the staff, the church program and the care of widows, orphans and needy families.

Tithing and Attitudes

The second scriptural principle concerning giving back to God has to do with your mental and emotional condition when you give. In 2 Cor. 9:7, Paul records:

Each man should give what he has decided in his heart to give, not reluctantly or under compulsion, for God loves a cheerful giver.

Notice that it doesn't say to give only if you feel like it; it says *when* you give, do it in a joyful spirit.

God wants you to give without feeling resentful, without reproaching God for requiring it. He also wants you to be able to give without bringing on reproach from another hu-man. Matt. 5:23 records these words of Jesus:

Therefore, if you are offering your gift at the altar and there remember that your brother has something against you, leave your gift there in front of the altar. First go and be reconciled to your bother; then come and offer your gift.

Jesus is signaling to us that bringing our offering into church is a part of our witness. When you support a church financially, you are saying that you agree with its principles and that you are identifying with what it teaches. If someone feels that you have wronged him—for instance, you owe him money—you will appear hypocritical if you put on a saintly face and go to church—unless you have first done what you can to make things right.

Of course it's important to remember that God is interested in you giving of your full substance—that is, more than just money. What else can you give cheerfully? Perhaps you could help a family with transportation needs. I also know a group of believers who give to God's work by "gleaning." These folks are not financially well off themselves, so they have taken the responsibility of rounding up surplus foodstuffs and clothing and stockpiling for needy families who seek assistance from their congregation. Don't you think God honors their time, effort and money spent on gasoline?

Let God direct your heart in the ways in which you can give cheerfully and without reservation; you'll be surprised at how He honors your giving and how your ministry (including your ministry of money) will expand.

Beyond the Tithe

The third principle is that you become more open to the direction of the Holy Spirit to help you "give as God has prospered you."

Paul wrote to Timothy in regard to those who were financially able to give more than the tithe:

> Command those who are rich in this present world . . . to do good, to be rich in good deeds, and to be generous and willing to share. (1 Tim. 6:17–18)

And what does Paul say about the Macedonians? Second Cor. 8:2 records:

> Out of the most severe trial, their overflowing joy and their

extreme poverty welled up in rich generosity.

Paul urges this witness on the Corinthians in verse seven of that chapter:

> But just as you excel in everything—in faith, in speech, in knowledge, in complete earnestness and in your love for us—see that you also excel in this grace of giving.

Giving beyond the tithe normally encompasses gifts to Christian organizations other than the church. But how is one to know if the so-called "para-church" group soliciting our donation is worthwhile? What guidelines do we follow in deciding to give beyond our local church?

Gift-Giving and Accountability

The first guideline is personal knowledge. Are you acquainted with the individuals involved? Is the missionary whose support you are considering known to you? What results are intended and what results are achieved? Can you establish personal correspondence and become a prayer partner as well as a donor?

Second, if you are not personally acquainted with the ministry, is the organization open about its successes and failures? Does it publish a financial statement and can you obtain one? How are its finances spent? What proportion of its income goes directly to the work and what is spent on administration? (Be wary of any group that seems reluctant to furnish such a breakdown, or of a group that devotes more than 25 percent of its income to administration.) Does the ministry show evidence of sound business practices? Does an outside accounting firm perform an audit of its books?

Third, find out who participates in the control of the operation. Is it strictly an "in-house" group who are themselves intimately connected with the ministry, or is there a separate, functioning board of trustees? Do the trustees enjoy a positive reputation? Are any of them known locally or nationally for being of upright character and sound business practice?

Fourth, how approachable are the principles and the trustees in regard to questions? Would an honest inquiry in the form of a personal letter bring only a form-letter reply?

Finally, how does the Holy Spirit witness with your spirit in regard to the contribution you are considering? If you have misgivings, consult others who support (or don't support) that organization and learn their reasons. Read the published reports and seek personal confirmation if need be. Spend time in prayer and see if the Holy Spirit will allow you to put your doubts behind you. If any doubt remains, hold off sending that donation. There is no lack of worthy, deserving groups you *can* support without reservation. If you were actually supposed to get involved with a ministry you chose to pass over, God will bring it to your attention again.

Remember What God Promises

Giving is an area in which God encourages us to test Him. Mal. 3:10 says:

> "Bring the whole tithe into the storehouse, that there may be food in my house. Test me in this," says the Lord Almighty, "and see if I will not throw open the floodgates of heaven and pour out so much blessing that you will not have room enough for it."

The refrain of this promise is echoed in the New Testament, in 2 Cor. 9:11:

> You will be made rich in every way so that you can be generous on every occasion, and through us your generosity will result in thanksgiving to God.

Remember to Whom Your Gift Is Given

The net result of giving must be to glorify God. This should be true of all elements of our lives, but tithes and offerings specifically fulfill this task. As Paul suggests, in 2 Cor. 9:12:

> This service that you perform is not only supplying the needs of God's people but is also overflowing in many expressions of thanks to God. Because of the service by which you have proved yourselves, men will praise God for

the obedience that accompanies your confession of the gospel of Christ, and for your generosity in sharing with them and with everyone else.

Finally, as Jesus taught, in Matt. 25:37, 40:

"Lord, when did we see you hungry and feed you, or thirsty and give you something to drink?" . . . The King will reply, "I tell you the truth, whatever you did for one of the least of these brothers of mine, you did for me."

Budgets

Considering household budgets is central to our study of financial planning for two reasons: First, if we are going to talk about saving money, it's necessary to know where that money will come from; second, the proper use of the family's spendable income is part of our responsibility that Matthew 25 points out.

Consider what Jesus said in another passage:

Suppose one of you wants to build a tower. Will he not first sit down and estimate the cost to see if he has enough money to complete it? For if he lays the foundation and is not able to finish it, everyone who sees it will ridicule him, saying, "This fellow began to build and was not able to finish." (Luke 14:28–30)

In this instance, Jesus was teaching on the cost of discipleship and about those who make halfhearted commitments to the kingdom. But His admonishing is not outside our discussion about family budgets at all.

What does it do to your witness as a Christian family if you are always living beyond your means? What kind of ridicule will you (and by implication, the Lord) have to suffer if you are late paying your bills, or if you have to juggle them from one month to the next, just one jump ahead of the collection agency?

What are the steps to having an effective family budget? I believe there are four.

How Are You Spending Your Money Now?

Before you can develop a budget—and long before you can begin using one—you need to know where your money is going *right now*.

To accomplish this you may need to keep a journal, actually entering each purchase as it's made over the course of a month. To this figure you'll need to add bills that are not payable every month (like the semi-annual auto insurance premium) and allow a monthly figure for that as well.

Don't cheat! Account honestly for every dollar. (Otherwise you'll end up with a miscellaneous category that is bigger than half your income!)

Here are the suggested categories:

1. Fixed expenses: mortgage/rent, property taxes, insurance, debt service, tithe, savings.

2. Variable expenses: food, utilities, medical/dental, clothing, maintenance.

3. Discretionary expenses: entertainment, miscellaneous.

This list is given in the order in which bills need to be paid: fixed, then variable, then discretionary. The object is to make 100 percent of your income match up with 100 percent of the list.

Allocating Your Income

After you've discovered where your money is going, the next step is to uncover what your problem areas are (if any). One of the ways to do this is by comparing your spending habits with a suggested budget. Please understand that the word *suggested* means just that; it is seldom possible to make your numbers conform exactly to someone else's concept of correctness. For this reason, the percentages we'll look at are only by general category, and are given as a range rather than as a certain figure.

Of your total income, the allocation by spending category is suggested to be:

1. Fixed expenses—50 to 60 percent.

2. Variable expenses—30 to 40 percent.

3. Discretionary expenses—0 to 20 percent.

The way to examine your spending habits is to compare your purchases in the reverse order to the listing shown. In other words, look first to see if the discretionary expense spending exceeds 20 percent of your income. If it does, you are undoubtedly in trouble in one of the other categories.

Next, review the variable category. Are there ways to save on your grocery bills? Should you become a coupon clipper? How about utilities? Phone bill?

When you examine the fixed expenses list, you may feel that savings has been incorrectly listed there. My attitude is this: after saying thank you to God, the next step regarding family finances is to put money away for yourself. I recommend this because many in our generation have become poor savers and investors, attempting to spend their income and save only what remains. Too often nothing remains. Other books on budgets and finances recommend 5 percent or even 10 percent savings. These numbers are good, but if they don't tell you *when* to save it, it won't happen. Better to save one percent faithfully every month rather than feel as though you should save 10 percent and actually put nothing away at all.

Okay, now that you've analyzed where your money is going, what's next? If the total of your expenses equals 110 percent of your income, what's the answer? We've already suggested that you may need to reduce your discretionary spending and there may be some savings that can be found in the variable expenses area as well. There's more good news too: contrary to popular belief, it isn't necessary to have *any* percent listed for debt service. (More about this in the next section of this chapter.)

Make Some Changes in Your Spending

It would be nice if all our monetary woes could be eliminated just by listing how we spend our incomes and comparing the percentages to some expert's recommendations. If this were true, successful dieting could be accomplished by comparing our weight to an insurance company's chart and wishing the numbers matched!

The next step to successful budgeting is to make the necessary cutbacks. Cutting a too-high grocery bill may be as *simple* as learning to buy your staple goods in quantity at the bulk-food warehouse. Cutting auto expenses may be as *painful* as selling that expensive car you "just had to have" and getting a cheaper, more economically feasible model.

Some books with excellent, practical suggestions on how to cut family expenses are:

Your Money Matters by Malcolm MacGregor
Your Finances in Changing Times by Larry Burkett
Your Money: Frustration or Freedom by Howard Dayton

Work Your Plan

The best budget is of no use if it isn't used. If you decide that your present situation requires that your entertainment budget be only 3 percent of your income, but you consistently find reasons to spend 10 percent, the budget can't accomplish its purpose. It's not that 3 percent is automatically "good" or that 10 percent is "bad." It's a matter of doing what's necessary to live within your means.

Why? Two reasons: Remember, how you manage your family spending is a part of your witness. Also remember that according to Jesus, being given charge of big important matters depends upon being faithful in the little ones. Think of living within your income as a training program in business management.

Besides your present-day witness, you need to keep in mind future endeavors, such as saving money for a future home, your children's education, or your retirement. Just like the corollary to Murphy's Law that says, "Junk expands to fill the available space," there's also a financial version: "Unstudied and uncontrolled, expenses always expand to eat up available income."

Small Hints

No savings in sight? Trying to save for a short vacation, or looking to find $25 per month to buy life insurance? Consider these ideas:

1. One soft drink per day at 60 cents is $18 per month.
2. One pack of cigarettes per day at $1 is $30 per month.
3. A car that gets 20 miles per gallon costs $13 per month to drive 5 miles to work, a 40 mpg car only half of that. Car pooling could cut it in half again, or even further.
4. Comparison shop your insurance. You may find $40 to $60 difference in premiums per car per 6 months.

Be creative! It's your money, your witness and your future.

Debt

More families get into more problems because of debt than for any other reason. I'm told that the majority of marital difficulties have financial woes as the root, or at least as a strong contributing factor.

Phil. 4:6 says:

Do not be anxious about anything. . . .

Few things are more grinding to your nerves than realizing your income is all spent *before* you've earned it.

Besides the debt itself, what about the interest charges? A credit card that charges 13.5 percent interest means you will repay $1135 for a $1000 purchase—*more* if the debt is not repaid in one year. Buying a home for $60,000 with a 30-year 10 percent mortgage means repaying over $200,000! The modern consumer has a fascination with credit (which should really be called debt). But what does the Bible say about it?

What the Bible Says About Debt

In Prov. 22:7 we read:

The rich rule over the poor, and the borrower is servant to the lender.

Scripture is pointing out that borrowing money means a loss of control—that the one borrowing is subservient to the one lending. How is this so? If you borrow using collateral—your house, for instance—you have pledged the object of collateral as security for your debt. In effect, you are no longer the owner of the pledged item until you have redeemed it by repaying the debt.

If you borrow without collateral, or on the strength of your good name alone, you are pledging your future income to make good the debt. Even though we don't have debtor's prisons anymore, failing to repay a loan still means you may wind up in the bondage of court action against you and garnished wages. You spend your life working for someone else—and that's the definition of slavery, isn't it?

God thinks that debt is a serious enough subject that the image used in Scripture to describe it is the same one used in referring to Satan's control over this world. This is so important a matter that we must digress from the subject of earthly financial planning for a moment to examine it.

Adam and Eve mortgaged their right to life in Paradise when they sinned. Since they were unable to repay the debt themselves, they lost their home. Each generation of humans since has been taking Satan's offer of "easy credit"—"buy now, pay later"—because none of us has successfully resisted temptation.

Except one person—Jesus. Even though He owed no debt because of sin at all, He paid with His life to redeem us from the power of sin ("the borrower is servant to the lender"). What's more, unless you take Jesus' offer of repaying your debt for you, you have no option but to let the devil foreclose on your collateral—your soul.

In fact, we are told in the book of Revelation that eventually Jesus will redeem even the world itself from Satan's temporary ownership when Jesus receives the scroll (deed) that only He is worthy to open.

If Satan still holds the deed to your life—if you recognize that you owe a spiritual debt you can't repay—why not take a moment right now to accept the offer Jesus is making to settle your account? Jesus has promised to accept the responsibility for your sins if you will say:

> Lord Jesus, I admit that sin has separated me from God, and that your Word says I owe a debt I cannot repay. Jesus,

I accept your offer to pay that debt for me. I want you to be my Savior. I want you and not Satan to be the Lord of my life.

If this is the first time you've prayed that prayer, or if you recognize that things in your life are not as they should be, please take a moment to write me in care of this publisher. I honestly believe that the study of your family's finances is an important one, but it doesn't even come close to matching the importance of your relationship with God.

Now let's resume our look at the problem of financial debt.

Don't Cosign

The second important point made in Scripture about debt is that you must not pledge yourself or your reputation for someone else. Prov. 11:15 teaches:

> He who puts up security for another will surely suffer, but whoever refuses to strike hands in pledge is safe.

Cosigning is not a mere formality, nor does it make you only partly responsible or obligated for one-half the debt. Cosigning means that you are responsible for the *whole thing* if the other signer defaults! Is it any wonder that Scripture teaches us to avoid cosigning? After all, we've got enough to learn about getting out of debt ourselves.

I have been asked frequently about cosigning for children or for elderly parents. My response is this: Just as the ideal is to not cosign *ever*, so it is true that the ideal would be for children or elderly parents to avoid debt altogether! Realizing that ideal conditions don't always exist, my advice is twofold: First, explore all other avenues of financial assistance—the outright gift of a vehicle for instance, or some other non-debt arrangement. Second, if the cosigning has already happened, or seems unavoidable, be certain that the value of the financed item *exceeds* the loan balance *after* the purchase. In other words, don't jeopardize your savings or your credit if a repossession occurs; be certain the remaining value of the purchase will at least satisfy the debt.

How to Get Out of Debt

The first and best remedy for being out of debt, of course, is not to get into it in the first place. Paying cash for your purchases is the only absolutely guaranteed way to avoid credit problems. If your budget doesn't allow for it, don't buy it. We have been sold on the idea of instant gratification, with 18 percent interest rate as the consequences!

This is not to say that credit cards are categorically bad. It certainly is a convenience when you don't have to carry cash for large purchases. Unfortunately, this convenience encourages the purchase of things we don't really need or of more expensive items than necessary because of the blandishment of "easy monthly payments." If you intend to use credit cards, make it your practice to pay off the balance *in full* every month. In this way, the "convenience" doesn't become a financial trap.

You will find that saving with a specific goal in mind and the attainment of the goal which allows you to pay in cash will give you a sense of accomplishment and satisfaction that far surpasses the "buy now, regret monthly" predicament of debt. (More on this in the section on short-term savings.)

When it comes to debts you already possess (and for purchases like your home which are not realistically settled with one payment), I suggest you follow these rules:

First, make the initial or down payment as large as you can. This practice will reduce the balance on which you will be charged interest, reduce the size of your monthly payment, shorten the time required to pay off the loan and increase the likelihood that if the item were repossessed, its value would satisfy the outstanding debt. Pay a minimum of 25 percent; larger if possible. The exception to this rule is home mortgages where 25 percent is not often realistic; in which case the amount should simply be as large as possible.

Second, always make more than the minimum monthly payment. If you elect to go into debt, budget for a monthly payment that is more than the payment schedule you are offered. Avoid loan contracts that have pre-payment penalties. Insist on the right to pay off the balance according to *your* schedule, not that of the loan company. Extended credit terms are a whirlpool of spiraling problems.

> EXAMPLE: On a balance of $900, a well-known national credit card will allow a minimum payment of $57 per month, of which $17 is finance charge.

> This means that even though the interest rate charged is 18 percent, the finance charge represents *30* percent of the monthly payment!

> Paying twice the amount allocated to the principal would pay off the loan in less than one year and would save over half the finance charges. (In this example $57 minus the finance charge of $17 yields a payment toward the principal of $40, so a double payment would be $80 per month.)

Third, on home mortgages, budget to be able to accept a 15-year-mortgage rather than a 30-year plan. The difference between the two programs is a savings of *$150,000* in interest charges on a $100,000 loan at 10 percent interest!

Fourth, to accelerate an existing mortgage, check your statement to see how much is principal and how much is interest; then on each payment *double* the amount you pay on the principal. (Indicate on your check and on the payment coupon that you want the additional payment applied to reduce the principal balance.) This simple expedient, if adhered to faithfully, will cut from one-third to one-half off the time needed to repay the loan.

Fifth, commit yourself to being debt free and set a target date by which you want this to be true. Cut up your credit cards if need be, and trust in the promise made in Ps. 37:3–4:

> Trust in the Lord and do good; dwell in the land and enjoy safe pasture. Delight yourself in the Lord and he will give you the desires of your heart.

Finally, once you are debt free, commit to savings the amount of monthly payments under which you had been laboring. Save for purchases so that you don't need credit; save for short-term goals and long-term investments. Fill up that emergency fund (as you always meant to do), so that the terminally ill car or the unexpected medical bill will not plummet you into debt again.

Concluding Thoughts

God delights in meeting your every need. What He asks from you is that your life reflect a standard of excellence that others can clearly see.

God doesn't need your gifts as much as you need to give them. Prov. 11:24–25 says:

> One man gives freely, yet gains even more; another withholds unduly, but comes to poverty. A generous man will prosper; he who refreshes others will himself be refreshed.

Keeping your expenses within the bounds of your income requires discipline and may mean strict adherence to a budget—but it will reduce anxiety. As Prov. 13:18 says:

> He who ignores discipline comes to poverty and shame.

Finally: *Avoid debt*. Stay out of it if at all possible, get out of it as quickly as you can. Remember the words of 2 Pet. 2:19:

> For a man is a slave to whatever has mastered him.

And those of Paul in Rom. 13:8:

> Let no debt remain outstanding, except the continuing debt to love one another.

At all times and in all ways make your financial decisions in light of how they reflect your Christianity. If you can say with Paul in Rom. 8:2,

> Through Christ Jesus the law of the Spirit of life has set me free from the law of sin and death,

then live like it.

Let your monetary concerns reflect good judgment on the name of Jesus.

Reviewing My Personal Situation:
Tithing

1. My belief about tithing is: (circle one)
   a. Both gift and percentage are required by Scripture.
   b. Giving is required but not a specific percent.
   c. All giving is voluntary.
2. Right now I am giving _____ to my church each month.
3. I am always/sometimes/never cheerful about giving.
4. God has brought a non-monthly gift to my mind. It is:

   _____
5. I feel led to support the _____ ministry.
   a. I have/have not researched this organization.
   b. After prayer, I do/do not feel comfortable supporting this ministry.
6. I have/have not successfully used a family budget.
7. True/False. Each month I find money remaining after all bills are paid.
8. The area of spending which is hardest to subdue is:

   _____
9. I am substantially/somewhat in debt.
10. True/False. I have debts that exceed the value of the purchased items.
11. I am committing $ _____ extra each month to getting out of debt.
12. True/False. I am committed to avoiding debt that cannot be paid in full each month.

PART TWO

RISK MANAGEMENT

4

What the Bible Says About Insurance

IN GENESIS, chapter 40, the story of Joseph in Egypt begins. We find Joseph in prison for a crime he didn't commit, demonstrating his ability to interpret the prophetic meaning of his fellow prisoners' dreams. Eventually, Pharaoh also has some disturbing dreams. When none of his magicians can interpret these frightening night visions, Joseph and his interpretive abilities are brought to Pharaoh's attention.

Joseph interprets Pharaoh's dreams as prophecies: there would be seven years of good harvests and plenty, followed by seven years of want and famine.

Joseph then suggests that Pharaoh prepare for the disastrous seven years by setting aside 20 percent of the harvest from each of the good years. Listen to how Pharaoh received Joseph's plan:

> The plan seemed good to Pharaoh and to all his officials. So Pharaoh asked them, "Can we find anyone like this man, one in whom is the spirit of God?" Then Pharaoh said to Joseph, "Since God has made all this known to you, there is no one so discerning and wise as you. You shall be in

charge of my palace, and all my people are to submit to your orders. Only with respect to the throne will I be greater than you." (Gen. 41:37–39)

Was the plan successful? You bet! So much so that when the famine had exhausted all the lands around, Egypt was still able to supply its own needs and have surplus remaining for sale to others.

The Scriptural Basis for Insurance

Setting aside a portion of your wealth in prosperous times as protection against future "lean times" is a biblical and ancient concept. Other cultures had similar ideas, even the Sumerians who had a form of credit insurance in case one was unable to repay a debt. The concept was further refined by the Romans, who formed mutual protection societies for such purposes as fire prevention, old-age income and burial expenses, charging each of the members a small fee for these services.

Modern insurance companies are only now in their third century of operation. Many scholars trace their formation to the group of individuals who met at Lloyd's coffeehouse in London in the late 1600's. These people agreed to *underwrite* a portion of any loss involved in the shipping of cargo, in exchange for a portion of the profits. Early in the history of the United States, organizations were formed to provide relief to the widows of deceased clergy and to provide an old-age pension to pastors. These groups later became the basis of insurance firms still in business today.

Since the word *insurance* does not appear in Scripture, what is the justification for its purchase by Christians? Is there a scriptural precept that permits or encourages us to take advantage of insurance protection? While no single passage refers to insurance, you find in the Bible a pattern of instruction leading to such an idea.

The Obligation to Make Restitution

Scripture clearly teaches that if we are guilty of damaging another person's property, or if we are negligent in protecting another's possession, we are responsible to replace the property or pay for it.

Immediately after Moses received the Ten Commandments on Mount Sinai, they were expanded and put into a form for practical application. One of the first subjects addressed was the matter of property rights, as discussed in Ex. 22:5:

> If a man grazes his livestock in a field or vineyard and lets them stray and they graze in another man's field, he must make restitution from the best of his own field or vineyard.

The owner of the stock referred to in this verse is *liable* for the damages. He is negligent, and therefore responsible to make good the loss. The passage continues:

> If a fire breaks out and spreads into thornbushes so that it burns shocks of grain or standing grain or the whole field, the one who started the fire must make restitution. (v. 6)

Doesn't this suggest legal liability?

Biblical Counsel on Prudence

Knowing that we are expected by God to make good on any loss that we cause should make a believer wonder how to prepare for such a circumstance. Even good drivers have accidents, and a moment's inattention can lead to thousands of dollars in repair bills and medical claims. Very few of us would be able to pay a $300,000 claim out of our own pockets. In the absence of that amount of savings and faced with a lawsuit for negligence in that amount, most of us would find it necessary to sell our property and our belongings to satisfy the claim. Such a danger can be avoided. The Bible teaches in Prov. 22:3:

> A prudent man sees danger and takes refuge, but the simple keep going and suffer for it.

A "prudent refuge" from today's disasters can be found in modern liability insurance. Most homeowner policies automatically include some personal liability protection, and for a nominal annual fee this coverage can be increased to $300,000 or more.

Faced with God's expectation that we make restitution for any damages we cause, and realizing that facing thousands of dollars of payments on our own is just not practical, an exchange of $12 in additional annual costs for an increase to $300,000 of protection seems to fall well within the biblical doctrine of prudence.

Understanding Insurance: Two Major Divisions

A fundamental understanding of financial management requires a basic working knowledge of insurance, and its two major categories.

Insurance protects two types of financial risk. The first is risk to property, including automobile, homeowner and personal property insurance. The second category of insurance protects against the loss of income, such as life insurance, disability income insurance and liability insurance.

Property Insurance

If you have an object of value—your house, for instance—that would be difficult or impossible for you to replace out of your own assets if it were destroyed, a logical step to take is to protect it with insurance.

The owner of valuable property can be protected against the economic harm that its loss would cause in any of a variety of circumstances. Typical hazards insured against are fire, theft, vandalism and breakage. To these hazards are added additional causes such as earthquake and windstorm; also secondary economic harm, such as loss of use.

In general, the more valuable the item to be covered, the more reasonably priced the protection. For example, a piece of jewelry valued at $1000 may cost $25 per year to insure, while a $100,000 home can be protected for $400 per year, or about $4 per thousand. What this comparison implies is that the degree of risk is a large factor in the pricing of insurance. The likelihood of losing jewelry is greater than the likelihood of totally losing your home. Premium calculation is also affected by other factors such as the variety of risks being insured against and the claims experience of the company involved.

We would all be much happier with the insurance premiums we had to pay if we went back to the original premise of insurance as protection against disaster. For too many years we have expected insurance to pay all of our costs after an accident or a loss, forgetting that these payments would come right back on us in the form of higher premiums. (More on this point later when we discuss deductibles).

Loss of Income

All of our future plans are made possible by income. Whether purchasing a home, saving for our children's education or planning for retirement, all are provided by income. Naturally, we would like to have sufficient income from our investments. Most people find that, for the majority of their lifetime, their income depends on their ability to work and earn a living. An adult's working lifetime now represents a substantial sum of money. An annual income of $30,000 multiplied over 30 years of employment comes out to $900,000! Notice that this figure was arrived at without considering any raises.

> Martin and Ellie McDonald are both 35 years of age. Their combined annual income approaches $40,000. If they never have an increase in pay and work to their expected retirement age of 65, their earned income will total $1.2 million.

Earnings in these amounts are not only blessings to thank God for, but a potential source of worry and something that needs protection as well. You see, there are four hazards that can interrupt the flow of spendable income or stop it completely. The first one of these is an accident for which you are responsible and which jeopardizes your future earnings through a legal liability. The second is an untimely death. Accident or serious illness is the third hazard to income. Accidents may bring high expenses or disability, sometimes called "living death." The final hazard is old age—the time when you are too old to earn, but not to old to eat.

While many people have considered some of the four hazards, most never attempt to coordinate a financial plan that takes into account all four potential hazards.

Concluding Thoughts

If you have any remaining doubts about the ability of insurance to stand the test of Scripture, or if you feel that spending three cents on the dollar to protect your income somehow shows a lack of trust in God, consider this verse from Nehemiah. As the Jews were seeking to rebuild the wall around Jerusalem, Nehemiah reports that their enemies

> . . .all plotted together to come and fight against Jerusalem and stir up trouble against it. But we prayed to our God and posted a guard day and night to meet this threat. (4:8)

"We prayed *and* we posted a guard!" This is precisely the proper Christian response to whatever would stir up trouble against your family. Seek God's guidance and then apply a portion of your resources to protection while your life continues to move forward in peace and security.

5

Automobile Insurance

LET'S BEGIN to focus our discussion about auto insurance by looking at a simple case history.

Gary and Hope Rutledge were cautious drivers. Neither had ever had an accident, and Gary's only ticket was received when he was in high school. Now, as their children reached driving age, the Rutledges constantly reminded them to be safe at all times, not to speed and never, under any circumstances, to drink and drive. Their children, who were conscientious and obedient, seemed to have inherited their parents' respect for the lethal force of an automobile.

The Rutledges recognized the need for auto insurance—yet they believed that any accident in which they were involved would undoubtedly be the other party's fault. Consequently, they carried a bodily injury liability of only $25,000 for any one person injured in an accident.

When their daughter Sarah asked to borrow the car to go to a school dance, the Rutledges made the usual cautioning statements, and allowed Sarah to use the car for the evening. Sarah's date, Bill, had already had a few drinks when she met him at the dance, but he seemed in control of himself. He insisted Sarah let him drive the car to the pizza parlor after the dance. Bill did okay at first—but on a dark, winding road, he failed to notice he was rapidly overtaking a slow-moving truck. Sarah yelled a warning, and Bill jerked the Rutledge car into the wrong lane—directly into the path of an on-coming station wagon.

Sarah survived the crash with facial lacerations. Bill suffered broken ribs and a fractured skull. But two of the four occupants of the station wagon were killed instantly. In the legal aftermath, it was determined that the Rutledges retained some legal liability for the accident since their car was the vehicle involved and since its operation was under the immediate supervision of a Rutledge family member who had given her permission for Bill to drive, knowing he had been drinking. The problem was compounded by the fact that Bill's family had no insurance and almost no assets. In the wrongful death suit that the survivors of the family in the station wagon pressed and won, the Rutledges' insurance company agreed to "go policy limits," which meant they paid out their full responsibility and were no longer involved in the affair. The final settlement exceeded a half-million dollars, of which more than $450,000 was the Rutledges's responsibility.

The Rutledges were permitted to keep their home in exchange for agreeing to a payment of $1000 per month toward the settlement, probably for the remainder of Gary's life.

Tragic accidents like the Rutledges' can never be prevented by adequate insurance, and all the money in the world will not replace a life nor make up for a foolish decision. As the Rutledge family discovered, however, the lack of adequate liability protection can prolong the agony associated with such a disaster and make the consequences even more far-reaching.

Many of you reading this may discover that your insurance limits are inadequate. This is because most folks find their policies unreadable or confusing, and they're embarrassed to ask their agent to explain something for which they've been paying for years.

Take a moment to locate your automobile policy. With it

nearby to refer to, let's review all the coverages, beginning with the *bodily injury protection* section.

Bodily Injury Coverage ⊀

Bodily injury coverage is the protection offered by your insurance company to settle claims involving medical expenses, loss of income or death. Most policies are written so that the protection accompanies the car, and therefore applies to anyone using the vehicle with your permission.

This is the single most important coverage provided by your auto policy, and one of the two most often required by state laws. Sadly, a great many people try to get by with the minimum coverage their state permits, usually expressed in their policies only as a pair of numbers such as 25/50.

These numbers express, in thousands of dollars, the following limits: the first number indicates the limit your insurance company will pay to any *one person* injured in an accident; the second number indicates the limit of coverage for *all injuries* sustained in the same accident. Many people are covered with a first-number figure of $25,000 or less. But how many bodily injury lawsuits have you seen reported in the newspaper that were settled for $25,000? It seems that almost all cases which go to trial are for over $100,000, and anything less than a half-million dollars is not considered newsworthy.

If you own a home, have any savings or other assets to be protected, or are concerned that you might spend the rest of your working lifetime satisfying a court-ordered debt, a limit of $25,000 is not going to cover you. The question, then, is, "How much liability protection do I need?"

An appropriate minimum coverage for this day and age would be $100,000 as a limit for any one person injured in an accident, and $300,000 for the total protection. You may, in fact, want to carry even higher limits if you can afford them. Protection up to $1 million or more is available, as we'll discuss later. You have no doubt noticed that the financial loss of the Rutledge family could have been covered if they had been carrying at least $500,000 of bodily injury protection.

This level of coverage may seem beyond what your family budget can afford; nonetheless I recommend you look into the level of coverage you *can* afford. Check your policy for the bodily injury figure listed there. Are you comfortable with your present level of protection?

The scriptural principle involved here is *prudence*. Earlier, Prov. 22:3 warned us to prepare as best we're able. Practically, this means collecting all the facts, like how much it will cost to increase bodily injury coverage, then prayerfully considering such a change.

If you're like most people, you can benefit from increasing the liability portion of your coverage, and it probably won't cost as much as you think, either. A little later in this chapter we'll consider a strategy for increasing your coverage with *no* increase in cost.

Property Damage Coverage:

Property damage concerns itself with the harm or destruction you cause to someone else's possessions as the result of an auto accident. We most often think of this coverage as applying to someone's car, but it could also represent damage to a plate glass window or a neighbor's rose bushes.

As was true with bodily injury protection, many people with a false sense of economy try to save money on this area by keeping their coverage to an absolute minimum—$10,000 for example.

Now the question is, how many new cars cost $10,000 or more to purchase?

If you are involved in an accident in which someone's brand new car is totaled, the likelihood is that $10,000 would not replace the car. Therefore, the difference between the $10,000 policy limit and the actual amount required would be your responsibility.

Again, a realistic and sufficient amount of protection is about $50,000. The possibility of causing a multiple-vehicle collision (or destroying a factory-fresh Mercedes) suggests that $100,000 might be even better.

Michelle Hardy hated driving in fog, and the fog on this December evening in California's San Joaquin Valley was the worst she'd ever seen. When she could no longer see two highway center line stripes ahead, she stopped her car.

Unfortunately, she failed to pull to the side of the road before stopping. The next five drivers had a chain-reaction collision, each crumpling the rear bumper of the car ahead.

Everyone had been proceeding slowly due to the fog, so there were no injuries. Because the other drivers had been operating their vehicles safely, however, Michelle's stopping in the center of the road was judged to be the cause of the collision.

Total damages: $30,000. Michelle had just taken her agent's recommendation to increase her property damage coverage to $50,000 after he pointed out that change only raised her premium $10! He was surprised when *she* brought *him* a bouquet of flowers and gave him a big thank-you kiss!

Medical Coverage

One of the questions I have been asked most often while reviewing an auto policy is why auto medical coverage is needed. The confusion stems, in part, from the fact that it seems to be much like bodily injury coverage.

Auto medical coverage provides the reimbursement of medical expenses to the driver and passengers of an auto involved in an accident, regardless of who was at fault. The policy also provides coverage for family members riding in some other car and even extends to family members if struck by a car. This coverage, unlike bodily injury, does not require that someone be found at fault, or judged to be negligent for payment to take place.

The Tone family had a child fall from their truck because of a door that did not latch properly. Fortunately, they were traveling at a slow speed, so Jessica's injuries were limited to scrapes and bruises.

Just to be sure, Jessica was taken to the emergency room and checked for internal injuries. She also had her elbow x-rayed and was given a tetanus shot.

The bill for this attention came to $345. The receipt was submitted to their auto insurance claim center, which paid it immediately and in full.

Medical coverage is usually written in amounts of $25,000 or less, and the amount you select should depend on your answers to the following questions:

Do you have health-care coverage and, if so, what is the most you might have to pay out of your own pocket for a claim? (If the deductible and a percentage of the cost had to be paid by you, what would the total be?)

How concerned are you about transporting guests who might not have any health-care coverage of their own, or lesser coverage than your family has?

Auto medical coverage can be used to pay the difference between what your major medical plan pays for the claim and what the actual total cost is. You should not be out-of-pocket at all if you have the two coverages. By the same token, if the greatest remaining cost to you would be, say, $1250 per person, it is an unnecessary expense to pay for $25,000 of per-person auto coverage.

The second consideration is the level of health-care protection carried by passengers who are not family members. For this reason, many drivers who often have guests riding along ask for $25,000 of coverage, but generally $10,000 is considered adequate.

If you are involved in an accident that is the other party's fault, their bodily injury coverage should be responsible for paying your medical expenses. If the matter takes some time to get resolved, however, your own policy can be used immediately under your medical coverage provision while legal matters are being straightened out.

Uninsured Motorist Coverage

Uninsured motorist coverage is perhaps the least understood of all the auto insurance policy's provisions. It does vary widely from state to state. Carefully read your policy and consult with your agent if your understanding is not clear.

Certain features will commonly be found:

- Uninsured motorist coverage applies to an accident in which the other party is at fault, but is driving without insurance. (Yes, you are paying for the negligence of other drivers. But taking forethought for the wrong action of others is akin to wearing a seat belt even though you don't intend to have an accident.)

- The limit of uninsured motorist protection may be as much as, but generally no more than, the amount of bodily injury coverage on your policy. It is expressed in the same form as bodily injury (25/50, for example), the first number indicating the per-person limit and the second indicating the per-accident limit.

State-to-state variations include the following:

- Some states have a provision called "underinsured motorist coverage," which applies to a situation in which the at-fault driver is insured but does not have enough coverage to pay all your medical expenses. Thus your policy would "take up the slack" so to speak.

- Uninsured motorist coverage generally applies only to medical expenses. Some states have a provision for "uninsured motorist property damage" coverage, through which the cost of repair to your vehicle would be reimbursed.

Here is an illustration:

Kevin Johnson's car was rear-ended while stopped at a stop sign. The guilty driver was found to be intoxicated, driving without insurance and without any assets or income.

Kevin's whiplash injury cost over $5000 in treatments during the following year. The entire cost was born by Kevin's uninsured motorist coverage.

Summary of Liability Coverages

The four coverages just discussed—bodily injury, property damage, medical and uninsured motorist—can be grouped together under the heading of liability protection. They all have to do with protecting you and your income against acts for which you are responsible, or the acts of others for which they are not prepared to be responsible.

Have you reviewed your present coverage while reading this section? If so, you have almost certainly found one or more areas that need to be increased. Before you become too concerned about increased costs, let me allay your worries. I now want to show you how to *save* some money on your auto policy.

Comprehensive Coverage

The next coverage that you probably find listed on your policy is comprehensive. This refers to damage to the insured vehicle caused by such diverse hazards as windstorm, hail, fire, vandalism or theft. It is almost always subject to a deductible, meaning the portion of the loss that must be borne by the insured before the insurance company gets involved.

The correct question to ask here is, *"How much is the right deductible?"* To answer this, we need to examine again your fundamental view of insurance. Do you want insurance to do every little thing for you, or are you willing to take a share of the risk? Remembering that the lower the deductible, the higher the premium, are you willing to have your insurance take care of only really major expenses in exchange for your being able to save some money?

Perhaps the best way to establish the correct deductible is by asking yourself, *"How much can I comfortably afford to pay out-of-pocket in the event of a broken windshield, or a fire, or if my car is stolen?"* If you can honestly say that you could afford $100 but that $200 would put a crimp in your budget, then $100 (or possibly $150) would be right for you. If, on the other hand, you could afford to pay $500 to replace a stolen vehicle, or if you could afford to replace a broken windshield completely on your own, then $500 is right for you.

The higher the deductible you are willing to accept, the less your premium. Under no circumstances should you take a deductible less than $100, for the premiums are ridiculously high relative to the additional $50 or $100 of protection you'll receive.

> The Miller family became concerned with the level of their bodily injury protection ($25,000/$50,000) after a neighbor with the same coverage had to take a second mortgage on his home to satisfy an accident lawsuit.
>
> After a visit with their agent, the Millers discovered that their present comprehensive deductible was ACV (actual cash value), or a $0 deductible. They agreed that they could certainly afford a $200 cost to them.
>
> Raising the deductible to $200 saved them enough money that they could increase their bodily injury limit to $100,000/$300,000 with no additional cost to them at all.
>
> As Mr. Miller remarked, "Better $200 out of savings if our car is stolen than lose our house if we accidentally injure or kill someone."

Collision Coverage

The sixth and final major coverage is collision. This is the protection you have for your own vehicle against damaging it in a collision that is your fault.

A deductible also applies to this coverage, and the same reasoning applies to collision as we discussed regarding comprehensive. You should always select as high a collision deductible as it is possible for your pocketbook to bear. I strongly recommend a $500 deductible as being the most economical; owners of high-priced or sports-type vehicles would do well to consider $1000.

I am often asked about dropping comprehensive and or collision coverages altogether. I do not feel that this is good stewardship unless:

1. The vehicle is so old or in such poor condition that damage in the amount of the deductible or less would cause the car to be declared a total loss, or if,
2. The vehicle is so unnecessary to the family that it would not be replaced if destroyed or stolen.

Otherwise, I think a better strategy is to raise the deductible as suggested before, until you find yourself faced with either of these two conditions. As a rule of thumb, you should consider dropping the physical damage coverages when your vehicle reaches ten years of age. But the actual decision will depend on how much value the car has left to be protected.

Optional Coverages

There are several optional coverages you may wish to hold. Generally, they are modestly priced and, depending on your particular circumstances, may be very useful. These include:

Towing—Reimbursement for roadside assistance. This coverage usually has a per-use limit of $50 or $100. It covers jump-starting dead batteries, changing flat tires and other mechanical aid, as well as towing. The cost is often so slight that one use in two years' time would repay the cost of the coverage for *two* cars for the two years.

Rental reimbursement—To pay all or a part of the cost of a rented replacement vehicle while your car is being repaired following an accident. Rental coverage is written with a per-day limit, such as $15 and a maximum number of covered days per accident—generally 30 days. Rental reimbursement is somewhat less valuable than towing, since it will not provide a replacement vehicle for mechanical failure, and families with two or more vehicles can usually work out some system during the repair time. The cost is from $6 to $10 per 6 months of coverage.

A Side Note on Rental Cars

The cost of renting a car for use on an out-of-town trip or while some mechanical work is being done to your regular transportation is greatly increased by adding optional insurance coverages to the rental agreement.

In most cases these are entirely unnecessary. Read your own auto policy and, if need be, consult your agent. Most insurance policies provide the same levels of protection to vehicles furnished for your temporary use as on your own cars. There is generally no additional cost for this courtesy, and in many cases the coverage furnished through your policy will exceed that being offered by the rental car company.

> *Accidental death*—Provides an accidental death and dismemberment benefit to the survivors of an auto accident. It is a little like betting on how you'll die, but it is inexpensive: $1 to $2 dollars per 6 months per covered individual.

And now, remember the Millers? Let's examine their story a little further:

> A further review of their policy convinced the Millers to raise the collision deductible on one vehicle from $100 to $500, and to drop the collision coverage completely from the one older car.

> The combined savings of these changes not only permitted them to increase their bodily injury coverage, but to also raise their property damage protection from $25,000 to $50,000 and to add both towing and accidental death to their policy.

> When all was said and done, the Millers ended up with more and better coverage, while still saving $40 every 6 months.

Calculating Your Auto Insurance Premium

Steps in Calculating

Automobile insurance involves such a complex set of factors that arriving at a rate almost always involves the use of a computer. So that the premium figure you are asked to pay twice a year will not remain a mystery, let's review these factors briefly:

1. The most obvious costs are connected with the coverages requested. Higher limits and lower deductibles both mean higher premiums.
2. The use of the vehicle affects the cost of coverage. Short mileage to work (less than 3 miles one way) and lower than average annual miles (less than 7500) will mean lower premiums. Higher costs are associated with busi-

ness use, or one-way work mileage over 10 miles.

3. The age of the driver affects the cost. Young operators (the definition may vary, but generally unmarried males up to age 30, married males to age 25 and unmarried females to age 25 are in the highest of all rate groups, especially if they are the principal operators of the vehicle. Remember, insurance companies refer to an operator as principal if he or she has full-time *access* to a car, not that the youth actually gets to drive the car all the time.

4. The make and model of vehicle to be insured affects the cost. Cars are rated for their cost new, their "damageability" and the expected cost of repair. They are then assigned a rating called a symbol code. The higher the symbol code, the more expensive the comprehensive and collision coverages will be. I encourage my clients to contact me when they have narrowed their search for a car to two or three choices. I can provide information on the cost to insure each before the deal is concluded.

5. The driving record of the family affects the cost of coverage. Many companies offer a preferred risk category to drivers with clean records and a higher cost standard rating to families with tickets or previous at-fault accidents. Don't take even one ticket lightly: the difference between preferred and standard may be a 60-percent jump in premium or more. Even more expensive is the sub-standard category.

In addition to the factors that are commonly used to determine rates, there is also a list of frequently available discounts.

1. The single most important discount is the good student discount. Generally offered to full-time students with at least a 3.0 grade point average, this discount can save as much as one-third the cost of a youthful operators coverage.

2. Many companies allow a driver training discount.

3. Some companies relieve the cost associated with driving long distances to work by allowing a car-pooling discount.
4. Several companies provide a discount to drivers in the lowest risk age group—45–65.
5. Some companies allow a non-smoker discount.
6. As discussed earlier, all companies allow a cost-saving for higher than normal deductibles.
7. Several companies now advertise a discount for having more than one line of insurance—for instance, both auto and home insurance—with the same company.
8. Finally, all companies of my acquaintance provide a lower rate per vehicle for insuring more than one car.

The important thing to remember through all this maze of charges and discounts is that comparison shopping is a must. Also, don't be shy about asking for a particular discount or cost reduction. Remember that the agent wants your account, and will be pleased to offer you whatever cost-savings you are eligible for in order to attract your business. Remember also that an agent who is responsive to your questions and is genuinely interested in your concerns, who has a reputable company to back him up, is worth paying a few extra dollars to retain.

Umbrella Liability Policies

We have referred to the fact that it is possible to obtain as much as $1 million of liability protection. This is accomplished by the purchase of an *umbrella liability policy*. Many financial counselors call this policy the best value available in insurance protection.

The purpose of an *umbrella policy* is to extend your liability protection beyond the limits of the base auto or homeowner policy up to $1 million or even more. For this reason, insurance companies require certain minimum underlying limits to be purchased before the umbrella policy is offered. This base amount is usually set at $250,000/$500,000 for auto bodily injury liability coverage and $300,000 for homeowner policy personal liability. Some companies will permit lower underlying limits, and these should be carefully considered, since their use would allow you to own $1 million of protection at perhaps no increase in your basic coverage. Some companies require that you have either the auto coverage or the homeowner coverage (or sometimes both) with that company before they will offer the umbrella.

In any case, umbrella liability policies are a good value, because their cost is right now between $150 and $200 per year.

Let's see how this policy can help a family like the Millers, whose case we've been following:

> The Millers pursued the idea of increasing their liability protection with an umbrella policy. They increased their homeowner deductible from $250 to $1000, thereby saving $100 per year. This amount, together with the $80 per year saved by the changes to their auto policy, was more than enough to purchase the umbrella policy at no additional cost to them.
>
> Now the Millers have $1 million of liability protection when they operate their vehicles and $1 million of personal liability protection as well.
>
> If they go ahead with their plan to purchase a boat, they will be able to give it $1 million of liability protection also for an additional amount of only $35 per year.

Automobile Insurance Claims

Although people like to gripe about the cost of their insurance, they don't get really angry unless they feel that a claim was not handled properly or that they were treated unfairly.

Insurance companies do make errors, and since they are run by humans, mistakes are bound to happen. Insurance companies are smart enough to realize, however, that they stand to lose more money through getting a reputation for dissatisfied customers than they could ever hope to save by deliberately quibbling over claims. Consequently, I doubt that most claims problems are intentional. They are more often the result of misunderstandings.

You can deal with misunderstanding in advance of the emotion that often surrounds a claim by doing a little study in two areas: the policy provisions and the claims process. Here's how:

> *Read your policy!* If a provision is not clear to you, ask your agent to explain. Pay particular attention to sections titled "Exclusions" or "Coverages not provided."
>
> *Know the policy limits.* Know how the value of your vehicle will be arrived at if it is a total loss. Find out what happens if you have a claim. Can you be surcharged and how much? When would such a charge be applied?

I learned my lesson about insurance policies the hard way:

> When my wife and I were newlyweds, we had the misfortune of being involved in an automobile accident. We were blessed in that neither of us was seriously injured, but the car was a total disaster and certainly not drivable.
>
> At the time, we were living some ten miles away from the college we were attending, and I had early classes four mornings of the week. We were a one-car family in those days, so I spent the next several weeks depending on some friends to pick me up and take me to the campus and home again at the end of the day. When that failed, as it did on occasion, I was out hitchhiking, trying to get to and from school.
>
> The car was eventually repaired and returned to us, and that incident has since remained in our memory as being an evidence of how the Lord provides in all circumstances because I was not ever late during the weeks of that unusual commute. What we didn't realize until much later was that the Lord had an even better provision in mind. You see, our policy provided for a rental car. Had we only known that provision existed, we would have had the services of a substitute vehicle at no cost, or very little cost to us. *Know your policy!*

The third thing you can do is know your insurance company:

Know how the claims process works. Will you be asked to obtain estimates, in the case of auto repair, or will an adjustor come to you? Is there a local claims office or will the claim be handled by mail and phone? To what extent will your agent be involved in the claim? Does he have the authority to settle small claims from his office? If you have a dispute over a settlement being offered, what recourse do you have?

Having the answers to these and similar questions *before* actually being involved in a claim will make handling the claim much smoother and more pleasant for all concerned.

Concluding Thoughts

After the purchase of a home, automobiles are the largest investment many of us will ever make. We not only expend hundreds of dollars on their upkeep, but spend a significant part of our budget insuring their operation.

The financial decision to purchase auto insurance involves not only the value of the car, but may affect the rest of our working lifetimes because of the liability question. Auto insurance is nothing to be entered into lightly, taken for granted, nor left unreviewed.

Reviewing My Personal Situation:
Automobile Insurance

1. My auto insurance is with ___Pemco___ company.
    My agent's name is _____ .
    My agent's phone number is _____ .
    I am/am not (circle one) satisfied with the service I am receiving.
2. My present bodily injury liability limit is _____ .
    My present property damage liability limit is _____ .
    My present auto medical limit is _____ .
    My present uninsured motorist coverage is _____ .
3. I do/do not (circle one) know how much it would cost to raise each limit in question 2 to the next higher limit.
4. My present comprehensive deductible is/are _____ .

My present collision deductible is/are _____ .

5. I do/do not (circle one) know how much money would be saved by raising the deductibles in question 4 to the next higher level.

6. My present policy contains extra features including (circle whichever apply): towing, rental, accidental death, loss-of-income, other.

6

Homeowner Insurance

MOST OF US agree that purchasing a home is the most expensive and certainly the most emotionally involved investment we will make. If a 40-year working life produces $1.5 million in income, then a $150,000 house represents 10 percent of our economic productivity—even more when we figure the interest cost.

So it stands to reason that such a valuable piece of property needs the very best in protection—protection not purchased lightly or without understanding. The key question is, "How can you pray in a thoughtful manner if you lack understanding of the issues involved?"

Most of us are aware that homeowner policies, like auto insurance, are actually combinations of several coverages packaged together. Let's spend some time reviewing these coverages.

Coverage on the Structure

Homeowner policies are principally designed to cover damage to the home itself. Beginning as protection against a loss by fire, modern homeowner policies offer coverage against a great many more hazards as well. These include damage by lightning, windstorm, collapse of roof due to the weight of ice or snow and water damage to the interior, to name a few of the more common problems.

Some less common perils you can insure against include damage by falling objects (crashing airplanes, for example), damage by motor vehicles and damage due to riot or "civil commotion." In fact, most modern policies are called "all peril" coverage, which means that somewhere in the policy there will be a list of those perils *excluded* from coverage. You can well imagine how important it is for the homeowner to be familiar with that list. Most people are not surprised that the basic homeowner policy does not cover earthquake or flood, but they may be unpleasantly surprised to find that their policy excludes coverage for "earth movement" or "faulty construction."

How Much Coverage Is Enough?

Most insurance companies provide a replacement cost rating service to determine the amount of structure protection appropriate for your home. Unless you are absolutely certain of the correct amount of coverage yourself, you should ask for assistance if your agent has not already offered to complete such a rating for you. There are two methods commonly used. The first is a cost-per-square foot method, and the second is a determination made by counting rooms and adding certain additional features. Both methods are accurate, if used properly.

Replacement cost has to be distinguished from market value, because homeowner insurance does not need to cover the value of the land on which the home sits. Oftentimes a good "ball park" replacement cost figure can be obtained by consulting a local builder as to his per-square-foot construction charge. This dollar amount, multiplied times the square-foot size of your home, should get close to the replacement cost.

Homes in parts of central California cost $60 per square foot to build. A 1500-square-foot home would therefore cost (1500 × $60) or $90,000 to rebuild.

Another method of obtaining an estimate of the replacement value of your home is to take its market value (what you paid for it, if it was recently purchased, or what similar homes in the neighborhood have been selling for) and multiply it by 80 percent. The idea behind this method is that the 20 percent of value thus eliminated represents the value of the lot.

A home that sold for $100,000 would cost approximately $80,000 to rebuild (100,000 × 80% = 80,000).

Both approximations must be treated with caution; don't rely on these methods alone for complete accuracy, since construction costs vary as widely as does market value.

Insurance companies that use either the square-foot method or the room-count method receive updated rating factors which take into account construction costs by zip code and are adjusted at least annually to reflect changes in the building-cost index. Even establishing an accurate replacement cost figure for the purpose of home insurance is not good forever. It should be recalculated at least every two years to stay up with current costs and help your coverage keep pace.

Insuring Less Than Full Value

I am sometimes asked whether it is possible to insure less than the full replacement cost of the home. This question is motivated by an attempt to save money and is based on the gamble that even a serious fire will not totally destroy the building.

Such a gamble invites disaster. Almost all policies require that a home be insured for at least 80 percent of its replacement cost, and many firms now insist on 90-percent or even 100-percent coverage. Failing to maintain the required level of protection subjects the policy to a *Reduction in Benefits*. Since such a reduction would not be discovered until after a loss has already occurred, it's best to not play games with the coverage amount, but insist on the accurate and complete protection of the structure.

Will and Andrea Moore, like many modern consumers, were appalled at the ever-increasing premiums for their insurance. It seemed that every time they turned around, the premiums went up—even though they lived in a modestly-priced home, drove small, economic automobiles, and had never made a claim.

Will's frustration reached the boiling point when he got a homeowner insurance statement that indicated the premium had gone up $30 for the year. The statement was accompanied by a letter indicating that this increase was because his coverage had risen from $80,000 to $85,000 on the structure itself due to an automatic feature in the policy which increased the coverage each year to keep pace with the rising building-cost index.

Will stormed to Andrea that this was an unfair and blatant way of wringing even more premium dollars out of their pockets and that probably $80,000 was more coverage than they needed, let alone the recent change to $85,000. Will called his insurance agent and canceled the policy, protesting loudly about the increase in coverage—ignoring the agent's comment that the automatic increase in coverage could be canceled. The agent was willing to meet with the Moores to examine the correct amount of replacement insurance needed and to adjust their policy accordingly.

Will ignored the suggestion. He began a phone campaign to locate an insurance company that would offer to quote him a premium on an amount of coverage he asked for, rather than one that wanted to see the home first. (Most reputable companies and agents *will* want to sit down with a homeowner and review the replacement cost required to make sure the home is adequately protected.) Will succeeded in locating a firm that quoted him exactly the amount of coverage he requested and did not ask to inspect the house. Will indicated the amount of coverage he wished to purchase, even though he knew the market value and the replacement cost of the home were much higher. He reasoned to Andrea that even if they should have a fire, the likelihood of the home being completely destroyed was very small and probably $50,000 was enough to cover any damages they would sustain.

Three years later, the $50,000 coverage was still the same, since Will had let his new insurance company know in no uncertain terms that he did not want any automatic increase. While the Moores were away for a weekend trip, some neighborhood children, aside from pilfering some minor items, succeeded in setting fire to the home. Will's reasoning was correct—in that an alert neighbor spotted the smoke coming from the home and a quick response by the fire department saved the structure, with an estimated loss of only $40,000.

What Will failed to realize was that his homeowner policy did not have a guaranteed replacement of the structure and did have an "80-percent insurance to value" rule, which the claims adjustor explained to him worked as follows: The pre-fire replacement value of the home was $80,000; to be fully protected the home should have been insured for no less than $64,000. Since Will selected his own insurance level, which at $50,000 was only 5/8ths of the replacement value of the home, the insurance company was only obligated to repair 5/8ths of the damage sustained. This meant that the Moores received a settlement in the amount of $25,000 and had to come up with a new loan for the $15,000 remaining balance required to return their structure to its pre-fire condition.

Will and Andrea learned a very expensive lesson. They discovered that while the $85,000 proposed coverage would have been higher than they actually needed, it was unwise to take it upon themselves to reduce the coverage to an arbitrary amount. Secondly, they agree they were unwise to not know the policy provisions as to how a loss would actually be calculated and the amount of damages paid.

A final complicating factor in the issue of structure coverage is inserted by your lender or mortgage company. They will always insist that at least the full amount of the loan be listed as the amount of structure coverage, even though the loan amount could and often does exceed the amount of the replacement cost.

Coverage on Personal Property

The second most important coverage provided by a home-owner policy concerns your personal belongings. The amount of personal property coverage is usually set equal to a certain percentage of the coverage on the structure. Most homeowner policies start this percentage out at 50 percent of the amount on the structure, but better policies have increased this figure to 70 or 75 percent.

> The Bensons' homeowner policy covers their home for $100,000 on the structure. It also automatically provides $70,000 of protection to their personal property (100,000 × 70%). This means that if their home were destroyed, it would be rebuilt up to the $100,000 replacement cost *and* they would receive up to $70,000 to replace their belongings.

I want to issue a word of caution here about internal policy limits on items in a high-risk category when it comes to theft. This limitation includes such items as jewelry, firearms and currency. If you aren't aware of such a limitation, then what you don't know *can* hurt you. You do not want to find out after a break-in that your $5000 of stolen jewelry was only protected for $500. It may be possible to increase the coverage on a particular category of item on a blanket basis without listing the individual items. Still, blanket increases often contain per-item limits, and therefore may not be adequate for the nature and value of your special valuables.

> The Bensons' homeowner policy has a limit of $500 for any one piece of jewelry and $1500 for total jewelry coverage. The Bensons considered a blanket increase of jewelry coverage to $2500, but discovered that the per-item limit remained $500. Since Mrs. Benson had a ring worth $1500, the blanket increase would not be adequate protection.

Personal Property Floater

Most insurance companies will provide a personal article "floater" (sometimes called a scheduled personal property endorsement), which actually lists the individual items and insures each piece for its own full value.

Such a floater often requires a current appraisal and can add a significant amount to the cost of the annual homeowner premium, depending on the value of the items insured, but this method is the only completely adequate way of protecting particularly valuable articles. Owners of expensive jewelry, collections of firearms or works of art should investigate the use of a personal articles floater. If you have unusually valuable items but are not sure whether a scheduled personal property endorsement is needed, read your policy's section on limitations and consult with your agent.

Jose and Carmen Sanchez had a lovely home in a nice neighborhood. Jose enjoyed purchasing for Carmen some expensive pieces of jewelry, including necklaces, bracelets and a diamond ring.

When they recently made a change in their homeowner insurance, their new agent asked some questions about their personal property in several different categories of what he called "high theft" items. When Jose questioned him about this, the agent responded that all homeowner policies had internal limits on certain high theft categories of personal belongings. He explained that this particular policy, while better than many, would cover only an individual item of jewelry up to $1000 and provided only $2500 of total coverage for jewelry. A quick consultation between Jose and Carmen revealed that her jewelry exceeded the $2500 limit by about three times. In fact, several individual pieces exceeded the $1000 individual limit as well.

The agent suggested that they obtain a "personal property floater" as an endorsement to their homeowner policy, thus insuring each article of jewelry for its own individual value. The agent explained that this coverage was not as expensive as many people thought and that their entire collection could be insured for an additional $150-per-year premium. This additional protection would not only eliminate the deductible from applying to the jewelry, but would protect the Sanchezes against even the misplacement of a ring.

The Sanchezes followed the agent's suggestion that they obtain a new appraisal of all of the jewelry and create a list or "schedule" of the pieces. The Sanchezes also decided to follow the agent's suggestion that they take the most valuable pieces, seldom worn because Carmen feared losing them, and place these in a safety deposit box. The items that were kept at home and worn more frequently were then insured for their full value at a cost of a little less than $100 a year.

When the Sanchezes' home was burglarized some time later, they were no less shocked to discover that the jewelry was missing. Nonetheless, they were relieved that their policy's personal property floater allowed them to replace the jewelry with no additional cost to them.

Replacement Cost Endorsement

Another important consideration in regard to personal property is the matter of replacement cost. Many basic homeowner policies require that damaged or stolen articles be evaluated for depreciation. Then that dollar amount is deducted from the settlement.

An appliance is considered to have a five-year lifetime, or a depreciation of 20 percent per year. If it were destroyed three years after purchase, the settlement offered would be only 40 percent of the original cost.

A good way to eliminate this trap is to insist on a replacement cost endorsement that eliminates the reduction for depreciation and even allows for the replacement of an item lost which now costs more than its original purchase price. Such an endorsement may mean an additional cost, but many of the newer and better homeowner policies include it automatically. It is something worth insisting on.

Detached Structure Coverage

Homeowner policies also apply a percentage, often 10 percent of the value of the structure, to a coverage called "appurtenate structure" or "detached structure." This is the amount of protection that the policy provides for construction not attached to the dwelling. Shop buildings, detached garages and yard barns would fall into this category. When adding up the value of detached structures to determine if the 10 percent figure is enough in your case, be sure to include fencing in the total.

Loss of Use Coverage

Another coverage often overlooked in homeowner policies has to do with the loss of a home's use during the time when major damage is being repaired. Also called "additional living expenses," this policy feature reimburses the homeowner for the cost of motel rooms and restaurant meals if the family has to move out of the home temporarily. This coverage is also expressed as a percentage of the structure coverage, often 20 percent to 40 percent. Better policies use the phrase "actual loss sustained," meaning there is no preset limit on this portion of the coverage.

> The Waterman family had a fire in part of their home. Since the fire damaged the kitchen and one bedroom, the home was not liveable until repaired.
>
> The Watermans received $1500 a month in living expenses for the two-month period required to put their home back in shape.

You should note that this is coverage for additional expenses beyond your normal monthly bills. It *will not* make your mortgage payment for you, nor pay for other regular expenses that the family would have had if the fire had not occurred.

Personal Liability Coverage

Most homeowner policies are issued with a built-in personal liability coverage of $100,000. Some older policies may still contain only $25,000 of automatic protection, while some newer ones may have the included figure set at $300,000. Any policy, unless already at the company's maximum figure, can have the liability limit increased for a very small amount.

> The Ajax Insurance Company automatically includes $100,000 of personal liability coverage with its homeowner policies. For $10 per year this coverage amount can be increased to $300,000.

This important coverage not only protects the family against economic loss because of accidents on their home premises for which they might be responsible but extends to personal responsibility elsewhere. Motor vehicle operation is specifically *excluded* from this protection, although some homeowner policies provide liability coverage for boats under a certain horsepower, or golf carts.

> Don Darcy was having a great time at a church picnic, playing first base in a softball game.
>
> In the third inning, he came to bat to hit the most towering fly ball of his career. It was not only a home run but went clear beyond the confines of the park—and came down in the middle of a passing motorist's windshield.
>
> The accident caused the driver to swerve, striking a parked car. Fortunately, no one was injured in this mishap, but there was about $5000 of damage to the two cars.
>
> Don's personal liability coverage took care of the damages, and it was possible in this instance to settle the claims without a court suit.

As in our earlier discussion of liability protection, even $300,000 of coverage may not be sufficient in this suit-happy society (although $300,000 should be considered a minimum). Remember that it is possible to increase your personal liability protection to $1 million through the use of an umbrella liability policy. (See page 79ff.)

Guest Medical Coverage

Homeowner policies also contain one other common provision in the form of medical insurance. This is usually a limited amount of protection—$1000 or $2000. It applies to the circumstance of reimbursing the medical expenses of someone who is a guest in your home and who has an accident.

The coverage for medical expenses does not apply to family members unless they are not residents of the household. The amount is set so low because this coverage offers to settle claims without establishing legal liability or responsibility on the part of the homeowner. For expenses beyond the medical limit, an injured guest would still have the same recourse to the personal liability portion of your coverage as anyone else injured on your property.

> Ray Moran was out raking the leaves in his front yard. His brother had come over to help out. Since Ray had only one leaf rake, which his brother was using, Ray was using a pitchfork.
>
> Everything was going well until they came to the very last pile of leaves. Both brothers were raking from opposite sides. Ray's brother made a move to sweep the pile of leaves into a bag; Ray made one more pass with the pitchfork.
>
> He speared his brother right through the fleshy part of his hand. The resulting x-ray, stitches and tetanus shot came to about $300.
>
> Ray learned two valuable lessons: Don't rake leaves with a pitchfork *and* homeowner policies have some important coverages besides fire insurance.

Optional Coverages

There are a number of optional coverages available to suit individual needs, some of which can be located with some companies for no additional cost and some of which will also be additional premium.

Earthquake coverage, for example, is available in many areas. This coverage can be a large additional cost, and generally has a separate deductible from the policy to which it is attached.

> Ajax Insurance will endorse homeowner policies to provide earthquake coverage. In New Mexico the cost of this endorsement is $25 per year on a $100,000 home. In California the same coverage adds $200 to the annual cost.
>
> In both states the earthquake endorsement requires a deductible equal to 10 percent of the damage (in other words, a $25,000 loss would mean a $2500 deductible), with a $1000 minimum.

Another frequently sought optional coverage is flood insurance. Homeowner policies seldom provide protection against damage by flood, although some companies do offer a flood endorsement similar to the earthquake coverage just discussed. More commonly, homeowners concerned about flood damage apply to the National Flood Insurance Program. Your agent should be able to provide you with details and can probably handle the transaction for you.

Some examples of optional coverages that cost extra with some firms but are automatic inclusions with others are

> refrigerated products coverage;
> stolen credit card liability coverage;
> business use of home liability coverage;
> extended liability to other dwellings;
> business inventory stored at home;
> theft of property from unlocked vehicles.

Renters and Condo Policies

Most insurance companies that write homeowner policies also provide coverage of a similar nature for families who rent and even to condo owners whose structure coverage is carried by their condo association.

Condo and renter policies omit coverage to the dwelling itself, and usually omit detached structure coverage also. From that point on they are similar to the homeowner policies discussed above. They are priced according to the amount of personal property coverage selected, usually starting with a $20,000 minimum. They often have two deductibles—which applies to damage to belongings, and a second, separate deductible that applies to theft.

Personal property coverage should be as important to a renter or condo owner as to a homeowner. Consequently, such a policy is worth investigating and purchasing. Two additional considerations would be the personal liability coverage included (and probably not available any other way), and damage to the interior of the structure. Many condo owners have been shocked to find out that, although structural damage from a fire was covered by their condo association, cleanup of smoke or water damage to the interior of their home was not.

Homeowner Claims

The satisfactory settlement of a homeowner claim depends on two factors: knowledge of the policy provisions and adequate record keeping.

Policy Provisions: As was the case with auto insurance, it is an absolute necessity for you to be familiar with the contents of your homeowner policy. Pay particular attention to any section labeled "Limitations" or "Exclusions." Remember, a home insurance policy may do more than you expect, like paying to have a paint spill professionally removed from carpet; but it may also do less than expected.

You will also want to become acquainted with the claims procedure—whom to contact, what to expect.

Of particular importance to homeowner claims is *record-keeping*. Remember that an adjustor will be working after a theft has already happened or a fire has occurred. He or she will be depending on you to furnish as complete an accounting, with descriptions, as possible.

> I was once seated in the home of a couple who had their backs to the fireplace. When the question of record-keeping came up, I asked if they could tell me how many items were on their mantel without turning to look. The husband said five, the wife seven. The actual total was eleven!
>
> How could these folks have told an adjustor *what* was lost if they couldn't even remember *how many* things were there?

Receipts for valuable purchases should be kept in a fireproof file or away from the premises. Photos of furniture, appliances and personal belongings, together with information as to make, model, date of purchase and purchase price are invaluable. Videotapes with narration are even better.

The satisfaction you feel at the settlement of your homeowner claim will be in direct proportion to quality of the descriptions you can provide.

Homeowner Premium Calculation

Don't be afraid to ask about premium discounts and credits. Home insurance is sold by professionals who are competing for your business. While you would not want to leave a company and an agent who have been providing good service for a few dollars savings, you shouldn't be shy about checking on prices either.

Some common discounts are:

New home discount—some companies will take off up to 20 percent of the premium for a brand new home, and smaller discounts for succeeding years.

Protective device discounts—savings as high as 15 percent are possible for a combination of smoke alarms, burglar alarms, dead-bolt locks and fire extinguishers.

Higher deductibles—The typical homeowner policy now has a $250 deductible. You can save as much as 25 percent of the annual premium by increasing the deductible to $1000.

Again, it would be prudent in the biblical sense to use your savings from these discounts to increase your liability coverage.

Concluding Thoughts About Homeowner Insurance

If God has blessed you with the resources to own a home, it makes sense that He expects you to apply sound business management to its operation. We are told in Isa. 32:18:

My people will dwell in peaceful dwelling places, in secure homes.

You can protect your home from loss by fire, or from having it taken away in a liability lawsuit by paying only a tiny fraction of its value in insurance premiums each year.

Be sure that you fully understand your policy's provisions, and pray carefully over expanded or optional coverages, so that you can truly dwell in secure homes.

Reviewing My Personal Situation:
Homeowner Insurance

1. My homeowner insurance is with _Penco_____ company.

My agent is _____ G.G Flood / Pemco
My agent's phone number is __ 628-4000 __.
I am/am not satisfied with the present service.
2. My home is covered for $__ 87,700 __. A "ball
park" estimate of the replacement value of my home is
$_____.
3. My present deductible is $__ 250 1,000 __.
My present liability limit is $__ 100,000 __ 300,000,
My present personal property limit is $ 61,390 __.
4. My homeowner policy has (circle which apply)
a. Guaranteed replacement of the structure.
b. Replacement value coverage of the contents.
c. Earthquake coverage.
d. Other special features__ silverware - 7,500, __.
e. Not sure.

- Raise deductible to
  1,000 ?
- Raise liability to 300,000
- Get Earthquake ins,
                126.00
              + ''
              ————
               137
              - 43
              ————
               94

7

Health Insurance

SOME OF US pay lip service to the old saying, "When you've got your health, you've got just about everything." What a large dose of truth is contained in that old maxim. Working to earn a living does depend on being healthy, and enjoying the results of our efforts is possible only if we stay healthy also.

Ill health is an unfortunate byproduct of living on this planet in our fallen condition. Don't we all look forward to being free from aches, pains and the common cold when we get to put on our glorified bodies?

Sickness and injury present hazards to our income, both directly and indirectly. The *direct* hazard is our inability to work and earn a living. Then we need to remedy the loss of income through an alternative source of funds. This is a problem we will address in the following chapter. The *indirect* hazard is the massive medical bills that can accumulate in such short order. Were it not for health insurance, the first major illness or serious accident encountered by a family would drive them into debt.

The younger of my two daughters recently suffered a ruptured appendix. She is doing fine, and recovered so quickly that by her fifth day of hospitalization, she had to be sent home; she was wearing out the nurses by running up and down the hall and dragging the IV bottle rack around after her.

Her hospital stay came to over $4000, the surgeon's fee over $1200, the surgeon's assistant, lab work and miscellaneous items another $500. Total: close to $6000 in completely unanticipated bills.

Many people feel confused by health insurance. They often indicate to me that they never know in advance what will or will not be paid. Such perplexity most often results from lack of a clear understanding of health insurance terminology. Maybe we should begin our discussion of health-care coverage with a vocabulary lesson.

Health Insurance Terminology

Deductible

The term with which most people are already familiar is deductible, meaning the amount an individual must be responsible for before the insurance company begins to pay. Deductibles range in size from a low of $10 to as high as $1000. The $250 deductible is increasingly common. Some insurance programs charge a separate deductible for every family member. Better policies limit the number of deductibles that can be charged to a family in a given year, sometimes as few as two.

Deductibles are generally good for a calendar year once they have been satisfied. You should be aware that some group plans might use a "plan year" deductible, meaning that a new deductible must be paid following the anniversary of the insurance program's inception. Also, watch out for plans that have a "per occurrence" deductible. This phrase means that a separate deductible will be required for each separate illness.

Coinsurance

Coinsurance represents the portion of the medical bills that remain to be paid by the insured party after the deductible has been paid. A common coinsurance arrangement is called an 80/20 plan. This pair of numbers signifies that the insurance company will pay 80 percent of the costs after the deductible, leaving the insured responsible for 20 percent.

Not all health-care programs are 80/20. There are many being marketed now that are 70/30 and at least one that is 50/50. It would seem that the higher the percentage paid by the insurance, the better the plan. This is not necessarily the case, as we'll see in a moment.

> Let's use $6000 as the total figure for my daughter's recent illness and surgery. Our deductible is $250 per calendar year per person. Since Ellie had not been sick this year before the appendicitis, the first $250 of these charges is ours.
>
> The balance, $5750, is multiplied by 80 percent to obtain the amount of payment by the insurance. Since 80 percent of $5750 is $4600, the remaining $1150 would seem to be my responsibility.

Stop Loss

Most, but not *all*, health-care plans have a *stop loss*. This phrase refers to a limitation being placed on the insured's portion of the coinsurance.

The stop loss can be expressed as the dollar expense to the insured (out-of-pocket cost). Or it may be written as the maximum the insurance company will pay at 80 percent before increasing its share to 100 percent. Or it may be explained as a maximum in eligible charges to be paid at 80 percent. Being clear on what portion of the medical expenses is yours will depend upon a clear understanding of which definition is being used. One must also know if the stop loss is per person or per family. (Note the cautions on page 104ff.)

Let's examine this by another look at our recent situation:

> Our family's insurance policy limits out-of-pocket cost to $1000 per person. What this means is that out of the $1150

balance at 20 percent, only $1000 will need to be paid by me. The other $150 (or any other amount that exceeded the stop loss) will be paid at 100 percent for the rest of the calendar year.

You should note that the out-of-pocket is somewhat of a misnomer. Since I had already paid the first $250, the actual cost to me was $1250, not just $1000.

Maximum Benefit

Most insurance policies now express their maximum benefit as a lifetime maximum, although some older plans and some specialty plans like dental coverage may use a per-year maximum.

Adequate coverage entails at least a $1 million lifetime maximum; $2 million is even better. The best plans available today indicate that they have an *unlimited lifetime maximum benefit*. Some plans are still being marketed with ridiculously low maximum benefits—those with $100,000 or even $250,000 limitations just won't get the job done.

> Nelson Brannum had never been ill for more than three days at a time before he collapsed with a heart attack.
>
> The resultant quadruple bypass operation cost over $45,000. An extended convalescence, rehabilitative therapy and constant monitoring pushed the total of Nelson's medical bills to over $100,000 in one year.
>
> Fortunately, Nelson's health-care plan provides for a $1 million lifetime benefit, so even though he's used a lot, there's still a great amount left. This is particularly important since Nelson's health history will prevent him from being accepted by any other individual health-care plan.
>
> Nelson's total cost was $3000.

Some Words of Caution

You may recall the earlier comment that it would appear that the higher the percentage paid by the insurance company the better. The reason this is not necessarily the case has to do with the actions of the coinsurance clause and the stop loss in conjunction.

An 80/20 plan with a stop loss of $10,000 in covered expenses means that the cost to the insured would be 20 percent of $10,000 or $2000, plus the deductible.

A 50/50 plan with a stop loss of $2000 in covered expenses would be a cost of only $1000 plus the deductible to the insured.

In other words, the 80/20 plan is better up to $5000 of covered expenses; thereafter the 50/50 plan would be better, *in this instance*.

Another cautionary note must be sounded in regard to some catch phrases used in health insurance policies.

Covered expenses. The expression "covered expenses" refers to the fact that some limitations exist in the policy. A treatment exceeding such a limit would not be deemed a covered expense. This means that the excess amount would be entirely the responsibility of the insured.

Unit values. Some older policies expressed the allowable payment for a given procedure in terms of "so many units" at so much value per unit.

A tonsillectomy deemed to be a five-unit operation would pay the surgeon only $100 at a unit value of $20.

Newer plans almost always express their payment amounts as "usual and customary" or "reasonable" charges. While it is still possible for a plan to come up short, it is less likely now than with the old unit-value approach.

Pre-authorization. Some so-called "cost containment" plans require a second opinion before a surgery is performed, or may insist that the proposed treatment be reviewed by the claims department for pre-approval. These plans pay a reduced benefit for services performed without the necessary authorization. All policies exclude emergency procedures from the rule.

Daily hospital charges. Again, older plans may specify a daily hospital-charge maximum. The better plans substitute a phrase such as "average semi-private rate" for a dollar figure. Pay attention to the "Intensive Care" benefit listed. If it is shown as a multiple of the regular room rate, it may not be adequate.

If any doubt exists regarding your present health-care plan, or a proposed medical policy, review it carefully with your agent. Ask for referrals to present clients of the suggested plan and get permission to contact them in regard to the performance of the policy in use.

> Chris Shumway had a hospital stay and surgery that came to $10,000. Since his policy specified a $100 deductible, which Chris had previously met, and a stop loss at $2500 of covered expenses on an 80/20 plan, Chris expected to be out-of-pocket $500.
>
> Imagine his shock when told that his policy specified a $150-per-day maximum and a maximum payment for his surgery of $5000, not the $8000 actually charged. Moreover, he was informed that since his procedure was elective and not an emergency, he should have obtained prior approval.
>
> When the dust settled, Chris's policy paid something less than half of the total charges, leaving him with a $5,500 bill.

Now you're probably thinking, "what a rotten policy." You may be right. The point, however, is Chris had been paying for this coverage for three years *without ever questioning its provisions*. Moreover, he could have requested a plan of treatment from his doctor and an estimate of charges from the hospital and then queried the claims office as to their payment *prior* to the operation. (That would have satisfied the preapproval requirement, too.)

Individual Versus Group Policies

Several years ago, the clear favorite was group insurance. At the time, groups offered more and varied benefits and were generally less expensive. This is no longer the case. Many individual plans offer options such as dental coverage and vision care, items that were previously obtainable only through a group plan. Additionally, group plans have gotten more and more expensive, to the point that unless an employer is paying all your medical insurance costs, you may find that a suitable individual plan is less expensive than your portion of the group plan costs.

There are still two considerations that clearly favor group coverage, if you are eligible. The first has to do with guaranteed insurability. Individual plans have gotten very strict about health history requirements. Individuals can be rejected, or certain conditions excluded from coverage on the basis of previous health experience. In the case of group insurance, employees joining an existing group (larger than a specified minimum size) are guaranteed coverage. Some people with poor health histories may find that their choice of employment is dictated by access to a group health plan.

The second consideration favoring group insurance is the question of maternity coverage. Since maternity costs are so high and since most individual policies exclude or severely limit maternity coverage, group plans are the clear favorite for this need. Incidentally, the best maternity coverage specifies that pregnancy is treated "as any other illness," which means there is no preset limit on the maternity benefit.

HMO's and PPO's

Health Maintenance Organizations (HMO's) and Professional Provider Organizations (PPO's) represent cost containment efforts through limited choice arrangements. An HMO operates certain hospitals and has physicians and other professionals as paid employees. Participation in an HMO implies the use of that HMO's facilities.

Similarly, but somewhat looser, a PPO is a group of physicians and institutions on an insurance company's approved list. Use of a doctor or hospital *not* on the list may mean receiving a lower benefit level than otherwise, except in the case of emergency treatment.

HMO's and PPO's may be excellent sources of medical care and save you health-care dollars, depending on the organization in your community. Some of my clients think that their HMO membership is terrific, while others feel that being limited in their choice of physician or hospital does not allow them sufficient freedom. Again, it is best to contact participants in your area before deciding if an HMO or PPO is for you.

"Specific Need" Health-Care Plans: Cancer Insurance, Dental and Others

What we have been discussing in this chapter so far is a good major medical program. A plan encompassing hospital costs and physician charges, without naming specific illnesses or conditions, is a major medical plan.

There are also specific condition plans being sold to meet a variety of needs, and we now turn our attention to these.

Cancer insurance is a program that pays additional benefits to those undergoing treatment for cancer. Its premise is that cancer can be so devastatingly expensive that regular major medical plans fall short of the needed assistance. Depending on your present major medical coverage, a cancer program might be a useful addition, but it can *never* substitute for a major medical plan. Many experts feel that cancer insurance is a waste of money if a properly constructed major medical plan is already in place.

Dental insurance is of particular interest to large families. In general, dental plans have limited benefits for the first one to three years, so that someone who has self-diagnosed an "about to be" dental problem can't run down and get the insurance for an immediate claim. Many dental plans have a per-year maximum benefit also.

Dental insurance can be valuable to families with children, particularly if an orthodontic benefit exists. Be sure to read the policy to understand such things as waiting periods and coinsurance figures.

Generally, dental insurance for a family costs from $400 to $500 per year. Taken together with a $100 deductible, 80-percent coinsurance and an annual maximum benefit of $1000, dental insurance may not be the bargain you think it is. Better perhaps to get the whole family caught up on needed work at once, then save the $400 premium each year for future fillings. You'd probably come out ahead.

Hospital Indemnity Plans pay an additional sum of money to an insured person for each day of hospitalization, regardless of what other medical benefits are being received.

These plans are useful for those whose major medical coverage does not adequately pay hospital charges and where the insured is stuck with the existing policy because of health reasons. Again, most people who can do so would be better served to upgrade their major medical coverage.

Conclusion

Health insurance costs have risen dramatically in the past few years. Premium increases routinely raise costs 15–25 percent annually and 40-percent increases are not uncommon. Unfortunately, health-care costs have also drastically increased, and few of us can afford the risk of operating without major medical insurance.

I cannot offer any solution to the rising expense, but I do know this: You had better make sure you're getting your money's worth. That can be true only if you understand your policy.

I also want you to know that I join the Apostle John in the sentiment he expresses in 3 John 2:

> Dear friend, I pray that you may enjoy good health and that all may go well with you, even as your soul is getting along well.

Reviewing My Personal Situation:

Health-Care Insurance

1. My present health-care coverage costs me $ _____ per month.
   My deductible is $ _____ per year, and will be charged _____ times for my family.
   After the deductible, my present plan pays _____ percent of the covered charges until the maximum out-of-pocket cost of $ _____ per year has been reached.
2. There are exclusions and/or limitations in my present policy. These include (circle):

a. Pre-existing conditions.
b. Maternity.
c. Vision.
d. Dental.
e. Prescriptions.
f. Mental health.
g. Specific physicians or facilities.
h. Other.
i. Not sure.

8

Disability Insurance

(on the job or off the job?) [handwritten annotation]

Best [handwritten annotation]

THE ABILITY to earn a living is not only a blessing of God but is one of the few things that Christians are encouraged to be ambitious about. As Paul says in 1 Thess. 4:11:

> Make it your ambition to lead a quiet life, to mind your own business and to work with your hands, just as we told you, so that your daily life may win the respect of outsiders and so that you will not be dependent on anybody.

It is the final phrase of that text—"so that you will not be dependent on anybody"—that supports your considering the purchase of disability income insurance. If you are not able to "work with your hands," then you will have to be dependent on others, *unless* you have either sufficient savings or an alternative source of income.

Many people believe that "someone" will take care of this need. If pressed they cite Social Security, state workers' compensation, company sick leave or personal savings. Very few individuals have actually mapped out a plan for coping with a long-term disability, the circumstances that some refer to as "living death."

Let's look at one case.

Ed Rode is 40 and a geological engineer for a major oil-producing corporation in the central valley of California. He is comfortably well-off and because his duties involve some field work in broken terrain and sometimes around hazardous machinery, his contract includes a generous disability income protection covering a substantial part of his salary for an extended period of time for any injury caused by an *on the job* accident.

Ed and Margie are childless and, though unable to have children herself, Margie's great love for children has caused her to volunteer for children's activities including Sunday school class, a Wednesday night program and volunteer activities at the local school.

When an insurance agent broached the subject of disability income protection with Ed, he brusquely denied any interest in the topic. He said he had no hazardous hobbies, that any on-the-job accident was well protected against, and that, in any case, he and Margie maintain a six-month reserve of income which he judged adequate for any emergencies.

A Sunday afternoon softball game proved him to be in error.

After a church picnic, Ed was taunted by some of the younger members of his congregation to prove that he was just as fit as they were. He was really going all out to show off to Margie and his friends that at 40 he was still "young." He was all over the ball field that day—hammering home runs into the outfield, chasing fly balls both left and right of his center field position and forcing the opposing catcher to make a hurried throw on almost every pitch when Ed was on base, since he stole at every given opportunity.

What happened would seem funny if it weren't so serious. Ed injured himself by stepping on a sprinkler head while chasing a high fly ball. The resulting slip, twist and fall tore his right knee joint apart. Months of repeated surgery and therapy accomplished two things. They restored to Ed the ability to put some weight on that leg and completely exhausted his accumulated sick leave. His company disability program provided no benefit in this situation since it was not an on-the-job accident. His inability to do the rough hiking and field survey work that his job required caused his company to offer him a laboratory position at a somewhat lower salary.

Ed and Margie are coping well with their situation. Though their savings are exhausted, they are able to maintain their standard of living and Ed, like the Apostle Paul, is learning to "be content in whatever situation he finds himself." Ed does not dismiss disability income protection lightly, however, since he realizes that had its benefits been available to him, it would have preserved their savings. Moreover, since he could not return to his "regular occupation," a disability contract could have continued paying him a supplemental monthly income even after he returned to work.

What About Social Security Disability Income Benefits?

Many people realize that Social Security does provide a disability income payment. Most are not surprised to find that there is a five-month waiting period before the benefit begins. Closer examination reveals that only about 30 percent of those disabled workers who apply for Social Security disability benefits actually receive them. Why is this so? The answer is that to qualify for benefits, your disability must "prevent you from being able to perform *any* substantial, gainful work and must be expected to last for at least twelve months or result in earlier death." In other words, you must be totally disabled, not just from your regular occupation but from any gainful employment. Furthermore, this disability, having lasted five months already, must be expected to last at least seven more months, or else be so severe as to kill you first! Consequently, some 70 percent of all applications for Social Security disability benefits are denied.

What about that first half year, anyway? I often illustrate the need for immediate, short-term protection this way: How long a vacation did you take this year? Why didn't you take a longer one, say three or even six months? If you answered, "Because I couldn't afford it," you have made my point for me.

What if a six-month "vacation" was not your choice? If

you were disabled and forced to take a six-month *unpaid* vacation, how would you and your family fair?

What Are the Chances of Becoming Disabled?

Before you dismiss the possibility of becoming disabled because you are young, or because you don't have a hazardous occupation, or because you don't engage in any dangerous activities, consider this: Every year one person out of eight will be temporarily or permanently disabled. During the same time period, only 1 out of 88 homes will have a fire, yet you wouldn't think of going without insurance protection for your home, would you?

older illnesses

Looking at the statistics another way tells us that your chances of being at least temporarily disabled before reaching age 65 are 1 in 3. Of course, the likelihood that you will suffer a disability from a serious illness increases with age. But

younger accidents

younger workers are not immune; it's just that a higher proportion of their disabilities are caused by accidents.

Let's look at disability income protection via another case study.

Mike and Janet Newton were in their late twenties and were extremely proud of the home they had purchased. Mike and Janet had been childhood sweethearts and had married when each was just 18 years of age. They had their first child at age 20 and purchased their first home that same year. Now, some ten years later, they had two children and a third on the way, and had traded up so that coincidentally they had just moved into their third home—one that would give them ample room to raise this young family.

Mike was very insurance conscious because of his family responsibilities. With the approaching birth of their third child, he had taken the initiative in contacting his insurance agent and reviewing their life insurance program. The agent and the Newtons agreed that all the life insurance was in order and, in fact, the agent complimented them on the completeness of their planning. He suggested to the Newtons that they might wish to consider some disability income insurance, since Mike, as a landscaper, was self-employed and therefore not covered by workman's compensation.

The Newtons asked for some more information about the program. The agent explained that a form of disability income protection called "non-cancelable and guaranteed renewable" would be just like their permanent life insurance. It would be inexpensive to purchase at Mike's age, and would lock in a premium that would never increase as he grew older, nor could the policy ever be changed in any way. The agent went on to explain that the policy could be obtained with a 30-, 60-, or 90-day waiting period and that, because of Mike's occupation, a length of benefit ranging between 1 and 5 years could be selected. The agent explored with the Newtons the amount of protection that they would need, beginning with the rule of thumb that he could offer about 60 percent of their current income level in protection. This amounted to about $1200 a month, but the premium for this amount was more then the Newtons thought they could afford.

The agent went on to explain that by adjusting the waiting period, the length of the benefit, and the amount of coverage, the premium could be lowered to fit in their budgeted amount. In fact, the next thing he asked was how much they felt they could afford. Mike and Janet conferred briefly and decided that they had room in their budget to allow a $25 payment per month. Mike added that this probably was not enough to do them any good. The agent politely disagreed, pointing out that their new home was obviously a great concern to them and what did they think of the idea of protecting the monthly mortgage payment. Together the agent and the Newtons worked out a program for $500 of monthly income benefit (just about the amount of the mortgage payment) that would last for 2 years of disability. Because the Newtons had such a small amount of savings to rely on, they felt that a 30-day waiting period was best for their circumstances. Even with this short a waiting period, the program as described cost less than the $25 per month they could afford. The application was written that same evening and just after the baby was born the new disability income policy was also delivered.

About a year later Mike was doing some heavy yard renovation that involved deep cultivation of the soil with a roto-tiller. When the tiller snagged a long-buried coat hanger, Mike stopped to remove it. Since the protruding wire extended above the roto-tiller blades within easy reach, he instinctively stooped to pull it free without shutting off the engine. The tiller flipped back into gear and the wire caught on the sleeve of his sweatshirt, pulling his arm down into the spiraling tiller.

Mike was fortunate in that his hand passed between the tiller blades and was not crushed. But the spinning blades did snap both bones in his forearm before he could hit the clutch on the machine. The doctor agreed that Mike was very fortunate that the injury was not more debilitating, but noted that Mike would have to wear a cast for three months and thereafter would need some physical therapy to bring the strength of the injured arm back to its pre-injury level. Because so much of Mike's work required the use of both arms, he felt a sense of panic at what would happen to his business, even though he knew that after the first 30 days their house payment would be taken care of.

As it worked out, God turned this accident into a benefit for the Newtons. Mike acquired a partner who brought with him a sizeable number of clients in an up-scale economic setting. Mike's new partner had the equipment and the muscle to be a good gardener but did not have Mike's flair for creative gardening and landscaping—something that the occupants of the more expensive neighborhood were seeking. The partnership has worked out extremely well, and Mike, after about six months, recovered the complete use of his arm. So business is not as usual—in fact, it's better than ever.

Mike and Janet do not pass off the use of the disability income insurance lightly, however. They note that during the first few months of Mike's injury, the combination of the insurance and their small savings allowed them to maintain a home and to continue eating while the partnership was getting established.

The Forms of Disability Income Insurance

Disability income protection comes in a variety of forms. It may be available to you through a group, or an association of which you are a member. These policies are generally limited in the amount of benefits they can provide. They usually permit price increases as you get older, and for the group rates to increase as well.

The very best kind of disability policies are those written as "non-cancellable and guaranteed renewable." This mouthful of insurance-eze means that once the policy is in force it can never be changed. The issuing company may make no change in the provisions of the policy features and even the cost is fixed according to your age at time of purchase. The company is obligated to fulfill the contract regardless of your advancing age or changes in your health, lifestyle or occupation. This last distinction is important, because someone who began a career in a relatively hazard-free environment may decide to change careers into something with a greater risk of becoming disabled.

> Bill Thorne started his working life as a schoolteacher. He purchased a non-cancellable and guaranteed renewable disability policy, not so much because he felt the need as because it was cheap. His young age and relatively safe working environment combined to lock in a low cost.
>
> After three years in teaching, a decline in the student population caused him to be laid off. Unwilling to uproot his family and move from the small town they enjoyed, he decided to stay and wait for another opening.
>
> In the meantime, he took a job as a heavy equipment operator for a local paving contractor. His disability policy didn't change at all. The premium stayed the same and all the benefits remained the same. In fact, it will stay that way even if he never goes back to teaching.

Basic Elements of the Disability Income Policy

There are five components that basically determine the cost of disability protection. Two of these cannot be adjusted; they are the age of the individual and his or her occupation. The younger the age at the time of purchase, the less expensive the policy will be. An individual's occupation is rated according to the hazards encountered and, to a certain extent, according to the expected income level of the profession. Occupations are generally grouped into one of five categories, although not all companies write insurance for all five categories, and all companies have an "X" list, meaning jobs for which no policy can be offered.

There are three more components that can be adjusted, thereby providing some flexibility in constructing the cost of the overall program. The three flexible elements are: the amount of the monthly disability benefit, the length of the waiting period between the onset of the disability and the first benefit payment (also called the elimination period), and the length of time the benefit will be paid thereafter (called "the benefit period").

The Amount of Monthly Benefit

As you can imagine, the amount of monthly benefit requested greatly affects the cost of the coverage. Companies also have guidelines by which they set maximum amounts that they will offer, according to a combination of factors involving occupation and present earnings. As a general rule, most disability insurers will allow a benefit maximum no higher than 60 percent of the individual's monthly income.

> An individual whose annual income is $25,000 would be eligible for about a $15,000 annual benefit, or about $1250 per month.

You should also be aware that the disability policies do not have to be written for the maximum possible amount, but can be scaled down to fit your budget. Many people believe that the primary obligation they want covered is the disability risk to their mortgage payment. This is a valid concern, of course.

Statistics indicate that only 3 percent of home mortgage foreclosures are caused by the death of the breadwinner, while 48 percent of foreclosures are caused by disability. In other words, a family is 16 times more likely to lose their home because the wage-earner was injured and could not work than because the wage-earner died. Many people find room in their household budgets to protect their mortgage payment against a disability loss, even if they feel they cannot purchase enough protection to cover the entire amount of income they would be eligible to protect.

What is the amount of your monthly mortgage payment? If you became disabled for six months or longer, could you keep up the payments? Have you ever investigated a disability policy? Can you think of any reason why you should put off checking into one?

The Waiting Period

The waiting or "elimination" period can vary from as little as no time elapsed between the onset of the disability and the start of the payments to as long as one or two years.

Most common waiting periods are 30, 60, or 90 days in length. A note of warning: A 30-day waiting period means that the first income from the disability policy will be received at the end of 60 days. The first 30 days satisfies the waiting period, and the insured becomes eligible for benefits; then at the end of another month the insured receives his first payment.

You can think of the relationship between the length of the elimination period and the cost of the coverage in terms of the deductible on car insurance: the higher the deductible, the lower the auto premium; and the longer the waiting period, the lower the cost.

After deciding how much of your income you want to protect with disability insurance, you can then decide how long it would be possible to wait for the benefits to start by determining how long you could pay that sum out of your savings or other resources. If you have followed the advice found elsewhere in this volume—keeping a reserve of from three-to-six months income—it may be possible for you to elect a six-month waiting period. This is a move you would find economical.

The Benefit Period

Once the payment amount starts coming in, how long should it continue? Of course, the longer the benefit continues, the higher the cost. Studies show that most disabilities last one year or less. Consequently, you may feel that with an adequate reserve of savings you could avoid the need for disability insurance altogether. If this is your thinking, consider that studies also show the longer a disability continues, the greater the reason to expect it to last longer still. In other words, those who suffer a disability and are not back at work in one year have a greater likelihood of seeing their disability stretch to two years; those who are still disabled at two years are likely to see it last for five years; and those disabled after five years are likely to be permanently disabled. Planning on a quick recovery and trying to save money by buying a short-term policy is a little like gambling on only having "small" auto accidents, or "little" fires. It would be far wiser to save money on the front end by accepting a longer waiting period than to scrimp on the length of the benefit. One is in your power to control, the other is not.

> A $1000 monthly benefit amount costs the same in monthly premiums whether it starts after 30 days and then lasts for 1 year *or* starts after 90 days and lasts for 5 years. Which makes better sense to you?

> Some insurance companies limit the length of benefit period offered by occupational class. In this situation, get as long a benefit period as you are eligible for, protecting as great a recovery period as possible.

Determining the Necessary Amount of Disability Protection

How can you determine how much disability income coverage you would need in order to cover you for more than a single-need amount—like the mortgage payment referred to earlier? Here are some guidelines:

1. Make a list of your regular monthly expenses, including mortgage or rent payments, utilities, food, clothing, insurance, credit card payments, transportation, medical costs, taxes, home upkeep and a miscellaneous category. ·

2. Eliminate from this list any items already covered by some form of protection. (Some credit debt may have a disability provision, for instance. Notice I say *may have*; you'll have to check.)

3. Add up any disability benefits to which you are already entitled. This area should be broken down into immediate benefits (like sick leave), six-month delayed benefits (like Social Security), and one year or longer delayed benefits (like a company-paid, long-term disability program).

4. Make notes on the amounts of benefits available, and any conditions or restrictions that apply.

5. Total up your available economic resources, including savings and other investments, your spouse's income and other long-term arrangements that could be tapped in the event of a disability. Make notes on any restrictions or penalties that would apply.

6. If you belong to a company pension plan, find out what provisions exist for making a disability withdrawal from the plan.

7. Subtract the total of available resources from total monthly expenses. If the remaining figure is 20 percent or less of your present family budget, you're probably in pretty good shape. (This is called "belt-tightening.") If your remaining monthly need exceeds 20 percent, then you should make a disability program a high priority to investigate.

Press and Faye Raeburn are a young couple of my acquaintance with a bright future. They are young, energetic, personable, and Press has been an insurance colleague of mine for some years. He is dedicated to servicing his clients' needs. It is not uncommon for him to work 12-hour days, and he responds to requests for information at all hours of the day and night. Faye helps not only with the household and their four children, but also works part time in Press's insurance office as well.

On a family vacation in southern California, the Raeburns' rental car stalled on the freeway. Press pulled off onto the shoulder of the road and looked under the hood to see if he could locate the trouble. No more than a moment later, their vehicle was struck from the rear by a drunk driver, traveling at high speed. The impact threw Press into the traffic lane where, by the grace of God, he was not struck by any of the oncoming vehicles. At the hospital, his iron constitution and God's mercy allowed him not only to experience a miraculous recovery but to leave the hospital and go home a week after an accident that would have killed 99 out of 100 individuals.

For the next year, Press struggled to put his life and his business back together. Since he was subject to dizziness, recurring headaches and numerous surgeries, he was not able to devote the time to his business that he had previously. His income as a self-employed person would no doubt have suffered had it not been for his disability income insurance.

After the waiting period was completed, he received a monthly benefit that allowed him to meet some of the additional expenses caused by his accident and to make up for any loss of income that he suffered. Press is now back at work full-steam and has recently taken on some new and exciting management duties for his company with a bright and promising future ahead of him. He and Faye do not hesitate to tell anyone who will listen what a valuable additional source of income and what a godsend the money was, coming exactly when it was needed.

Contract "Language"

When examining a proposed disability-income policy, be sure to read carefully the "Definition of Disability." This important contract provision is what determines whether you are eligible for a benefit payment. Some disability policies require you to be bedridden, hospitalized or totally incapable of income-producing activities *before* you are considered disabled.

As we have seen, this is precisely the reason why so many requests for Social Security benefits are denied; it would be terrible to fall into a similar trap on a privately owned plan.

The very best definitions of disability refer to your inability to work in your own "regular" occupation. This means that you are considered to be disabled if you cannot continue full time in your present position. Some policies provide a split definition, referring to your regular occupation for a certain period of time and any gainful work (or another similar phrase) thereafter.

> Ajax Insurance sells a disability program which states that one is considered totally disabled if "unable to perform the substantial and material duties of your regular occupation for a period of two years, or if unable to perform the substantial and material duties of an occupation reasonable for your education and training thereafter."

If you are unclear as to the meaning of the definition of disability being used, ask the agent for an explanation.

Some companies refer to the definition of disability in terms of lost or reduced income. This sort of standard works well for some professions, but might be difficult to apply to someone self-employed, whose professional expertise and employment make it hard to distinguish between business and personal income.

Optional Disability Benefits

Buying a disability policy is much like shopping for a new car: you can get a stripped-down model, which provides decent transportation, or you can purchase one that's "loaded with all the extras."

This is not to say that the optional disability coverages are not worthy of your consideration. In particular, the ones we will discuss now are those most frequently requested:

Residual benefits—The word residual, used in connection with disability insurance, means the same as partial disability benefits. This means that if you are able to do some of the duties of your profession, or all the duties of your profession, *but not full time*, you are entitled to a proportion of the monthly benefit. Some companies require that you be totally disabled before a partial benefit payment will be made. Other companies will allow any combination of total or partial disability to satisfy the waiting period. This feature is of particular interest to professionals such as physicians and attorneys, since a disability in their situations might mean not being able to keep as intense a schedule as they did previously.

Shane Duffy is a young accountant. He has often advised business owners about the need to protect themselves against disability with a personal disability income policy, or a business overhead expense policy. Since Shane belongs to both the state and national association of his profession and participates in their group disability plan, he never felt the need to purchase a personal disability income policy for himself.

After Shane suffered a detached retina, which was repaired by laser surgery, he was back at work in only two weeks. He was cautioned by his ophthalmologist, however, to limit himself to eight hours per day to avoid straining the newly repaired eye. This was in sharp contrast to the 14-hour days that Shane had been accustomed to working and consequently caused a severe cutback in the expansion of his business. You can imagine Shane's dismay when he discovered that his association disability policy only paid a benefit for total disability, and since he was back at work in some capacity after such a short period of time, the waiting period was not even satisfied. The association policy paid no benefit whatsoever.

After 18 months, Shane is completely recovered and working his old schedule again. You can believe that now he owns a personal disability policy which includes a partial disability benefit (often called residual benefit), and that he recommends such a policy to other professional associates and to other professionals whose livelihood depends completely on their ability to perform at 100 percent of their capacity unless some substitute income is available.

Cost of living adjustment—A cost of living adjustment (COLA) is an often-requested option to a disability policy. It provides that a disability benefit will keep pace with increasing prices, rather than remaining fixed. It is valuable on five-year or longer benefit periods, but not as important on lesser length benefits.

Guaranteed insurability—Many people who are at the beginning of their careers expect that their incomes will increase as their profession develops. Consequently, they expect to need larger disability benefit amounts in future years. Since purchasing a disability policy requires that you be in good health, this is a way of circumventing that requirement at some future, as yet unknown, date; in effect, you are insuring your insurability. It means that the insurance company guarantees you the right to purchase additional insurance, regardless of the condition of your health.

There are numerous other disability plan options. Some of them provide "first day" benefits, meaning a waiver of the waiting period. Others permit you to hope for a Social Security benefit while giving you a "contingency" benefit to fall back on in case Social Security doesn't come through. These and still other options need to be evaluated in the light of your individual situation.

Concluding Thoughts

Disability policies need not be confusing or mysterious. They provide a very real benefit by way of making possible a replacement income at the time when it is most needed, helping you to remain independent of others.

In simplest terms, they consist of a monthly benefit amount, which can be adjusted to fit your needs, as can the waiting time before the benefit starts and the duration it continues once it has begun. They can be constructed to take care of a specific need such as a mortgage payment, or broad enough to encompass a sizeable amount of your monthly budget. Plans can even be tailored to suit your individual needs, with a range of optional provisions.

It is a paradox that loss of income because of serious accident or illness is such a very real possibility, while disability income protection is one of the least purchased and most neglected of all insurance programs.

A few dollars, wisely spent, may provide thousands of dollars worth of peace of mind. And while you and I both know that peace of mind comes from God, He has also enabled us to make wise choices concerning protection for our ability to work and earn a living. Personally, I thank Him for that provision, just as I thank Him for His other blessings. I keep in mind the words of Solomon in Eccles. 5:19:

> Moreover, when God gives any man wealth and possessions, and enables him to enjoy them, to accept his lot and be happy in his work—this is a gift of God.

A Comparison of Possible Disasters

The chances in one year of . . .[1]	*Are . . .*
1. your house having a fire	1 in 87
2. your being in a car accident	1 in 77
3. your being disabled for at least 3 months	1 in 8

Chances of Being Disabled for at Least 6 Months Prior to Age 65[2]

If worker is now age . . .	*Number out of 100 who will be disabled is . . .*
25	34
30	33
35	33
40	32
45	30
50	28
	(about 1 out of 3)

---

[1]Monarch Insurance Co.
[2]National Underwriter Company

Chances of Being Disabled for Two or More Years Prior to Age 65[3]

If worker is now age . . .	Number out of 100 who will be disabled is . . .
25	22
30	22
35	21
40	21
45	20
50	10
	(About 1 out of 5)

Reviewing My Personal Situation:
Disability Insurance

1. I presently have/don't have disability income insurance.
2. The coverage I Have:
   a. I own myself.
   b. Is furnished by my employment.
   c. Both.
3. The coverage I have from work:
   a. Only covers work-related injury.
   b. Covers both on- and off-work injury.
   c. Not sure.
4. The monthly benefit available to me from all known sources of disability protection is $_____ .
5. My family would have at least $_____ of monthly income.
6. I think an appropriate amount of disability income protection for me would be:
   a. $_____ per month;
   b. beginning after _____ days of disability;
   c. lasting for _____ months of disability.

---

[3]National Underwriter Company

9

Life Insurance Policies

EVERYONE WANTS to sell you life insurance today—
the agent who insures your home, the bank that holds your
mortgage, your best friend who wants to show you "a new
idea," even the ad in the Sunday supplement to your newspaper. Your credit card company will sell you life insurance.
So will the department store where you shop and the frater-
nal organization that wants you as a member.

Is it any wonder the American public looks at life insurance and its promoters with such a jaundiced eye? How can
you sort through all the competing claims, and what is all the
fuss about anyway? If it's just a matter of burial costs, why
not prepay them and have done with it?

I honestly believe, however, that life insurance is one of
the greatest human inventions.

When I was a young insurance agent I was called on to
handle a death claim. It seems that a law enforcement officer, not much older than I, had been killed in a crash while
trying to apprehend a drunk driver.

His widow had discovered a policy, the existence of which
she had not known about. Since it was in with some papers

129

from his law enforcement officers' association, she called them first and they contacted me.

We had been invited by the association to review their members' employment benefits and to offer each one a payroll-deduction life insurance plan. This officer had agreed to the deduction of $5 per week. When the policy was delivered he had filed it away, without even telling his wife.

The young widow did not *know* what the policy was worth. You can only guess her astonishment when I returned to her home one week later with a check for $96,000! Because of the officer's youth and the inclusion of an accidental death benefit, his $5 per week payment had brought his family a substantial sum of money.

Not just substantial; critical. The young widow recounted to me in tears how they had just bought a new home with an enormous mortgage, how they had two young children and how she had not worked outside the home in eight years.

What she was saying was that she didn't *know* how she was going to keep the home had this unexpected blessing not come to light.

Would this story have been as dramatic if the officer had not died? Probably not, although infinitely happier. All the money in the world won't replace that husband and father. And yet the life insurance policy would still have been a valuable addition to that family's life.

In 10 years, it would have provided a few thousand dollars of cash value to launch a child's college plans. In 20, it could have paid the costs of a wedding. In 30, it would have been worth three times as much in cash value as had been paid in. In 35 it could have been surrendered in exchange for a lifetime monthly income.

Let's push the selling of life insurance aside for a time and look at this marvel itself.

Singles and Life Insurance

Many single folks feel that since they have no spouse dependent upon them for support, they have no need for life insurance. This attitude should not apply to a single *parent*, because the need for life insurance is even *more* critical. Similarly, a single person who is responsible for elderly parents or other dependent relatives would not want to omit studying the valuable protection offered by life insurance.

But what about those who have no dependents who would suffer economic hardship in the event of their death? As I see it, there are still three good reasons for single folks to study and apply the lessons of life insurance:

1. Undoubtedly, an unexpected death will leave some unpaid bills; some financial responsibilities. What about those who survive you? Who will be billed for remaining debts, unpaid medical expenses and funeral costs? In short, the section on "Cost Needs at Death" will still apply to you.

2. Second, permanent life insurance, purchased when you are relatively young, locks in a lifetime guaranteed premium. Even if you felt no "need" for the policy for twenty years, its cost would still be only what it was two decades before.
   More important is the question of *insurability*. Purchasing life insurance when you are physically able guarantees that the policy will exist when your dependents increase, even if you are then unable to qualify for it.

3. Modern cash-value policies provide valuable tax-savings features. These qualities should be of as much interest to the single investor as to the married (perhaps more so because of the possible greater savings which can be set aside).

The whole subject of "singleness" and insurance and investing requires more specific attention to detail than we can devote here. I believe that singles will find the broad principles depicted in this volume to be helpful, even if not directed precisely to their needs.

What Is Life Insurance?

Life insurance is money for sale. For about 3 cents on the dollar per year, a family can instantly possess a $50,000 or

$100,000 estate. You see, the greatest enemy to your family's financial security is time, or rather the uncertainty about how much time we have on this earth.

If I live and am allowed to work and support my family—then praise God!—I know that my family's needs will be met. We will work through children outgrowing their clothes, buying a home, paying for auto insurance, planning for college and all the myriad needs a family has.

But what if I'm suddenly *not* around to provide for my family? What if all the future plans that required my income were suddenly in jeopardy because the key component were removed?

If I live and work another 30 years, my income made (and spent) may be $1 million or more. Life insurance gives me the ability to *guarantee* that sum (or a significant part of it) will be available to my family. Moreover, it will be *immediately available* if I were to suddenly pass away.

If this "death protection" were all that life insurance did, it would still be a marvel, and of paramount importance to families who care about seeing their dreams fulfilled. But life insurance is much more than just "death protection."

There are other types of cash reserves made available by life insurance besides the one in time of death. These are: the accumulated cash value available in the form of loans during the policy's existence, and retirement income if the need for death protection has passed.

In recent years, cash value life insurance has gotten even more exciting. Modern cash value policies compete very favorably with other savings programs. In fact, recent experience has shown that cash value accumulates at rates 3 percent to 6 percent better than bank passbook savings, 2 percent to 5 percent better than money market funds, and 1 percent to 2 percent better than certificates of deposit. How important is a one or two percent difference? (Read the upcoming discussion of compound interest on p. 177ff. and you'll see.)

Moreover, the cash values in life insurance policies grow tax deferred. This means that the interest earned is not subject to current income tax, as are all three other savings listed above. Instead, life insurance cash values are not taxed until withdrawn. (See page 135ff.)

What this means is that life insurance, besides protecting your family against the economic tragedy they would suffer if you died, also represents a truly fantastic place to accumulate cash reserves. In fact, modern life insurance policies have been called "tax-favored plans for creating a cash reserve with an important death benefit as well."

> Max Johnson is getting ready to retire next year. He took out cash value life insurance when he and Judy were first married, and added another policy when each of their two children arrived. Max added a fourth policy when they bought their "dream house."
>
> Over the years, Max and Judy borrowed against their cash value reserve, finding the 6-percent interest they were charged a better deal than was possible elsewhere.
>
> They watched the cash values grow according to the guarantee in the policy and noticed how their premium payment (which never changed over the years) seemed to shrink to insignificance.
>
> When their agent introduced them to the new "universal life" policy, they saw the advantages immediately. They combined all their four policies into one universal life plan and watched their cash values soar as the interest rate earned went from 5 percent to 9 percent. Max's payment didn't increase at all, but he liked the interest rate (tax deferred) so much that he elected to deposit additional sums.
>
> Now he's ready to retire. Max and Judy thank God that they have lived to retire together. They also thank God for the wisdom and forethought they had to purchase cash value life insurance. Max will be taking a completely paid up policy with part of the cash values, and drawing a lifetime monthly income from the rest.

The Scriptural Basis for Life Insurance

Is there a basis in Scripture to justify the purchase of life insurance? After all, I'm not supposed to worry about what tomorrow brings, so how can I justify trying to prepare for needs that won't even exist until after my death?

The Bible indirectly refers to life insurance in a message by Paul found in First Timothy. In this passage Paul reviews the responsibility of the church in caring for widows and orphans. He makes it clear that the family of the bereaved has the primary responsibility, ahead of the church's role. In fact, he says in 1 Tim. 5:3–4:

> Give proper recognition to those widows who are really in need. But if a widow has children or grandchildren, these should learn first of all to put their religion into practice by caring for their own family and so repaying their parents and grandparents, for this is pleasing to God.

Now you may be thinking this passage seems to eliminate any basis for life insurance, since it suggests that the family has the duty of providing for a widowed mother and that, thereafter, it's the church's job. Let's read on in First Timothy 5:

> If anyone does not provide for his relatives, and especially for his immediate family, he has denied the faith and is worse than an unbeliever. (v. 8)

Now this admonishment is intended to reinforce the command to take care of your own, but it also introduces an interesting thought. Through the use of life insurance, it is possible to provide for your relatives even after your death. The miracle of life insurance is that a little forethought and provision now can *greatly* relieve desperate family concerns in the event of your untimely death.

We realize of course that no one is immune to death. Intellectually we acknowledge that God measures our life spans and that nothing we do extends our time on this earth. And yet, life insurance, as a topic, makes many folks uncomfortable. It reminds us of our mortality when we would prefer to think of tragedy as happening to "the other guy."

Let's examine the subject to see if we can make sense out of the rain of life insurance choices with which we are pelted.

Different Types of Life Insurance

How many kinds of life insurance have you heard of? "Whole life" and "term," "paid up" and "annually renewable," "mortgage life" and "par plans," "vanishing premium" and "universal life"! Is there any wonder so much confusion exists? In their race to catch the attention of the insurance-buying public, insurance companies have created a hodge-podge of phrases that you'd need to have an insurance agent permanently at hand to explain.

To begin with, life insurance can be broadly classified into just two types: those that build a cash reserve and those that do not. Any policy that lacks a cash value reserve can be called "term." They come in many varieties, with catchy (or confusing) names, but they all have some traits in common.

First, all term insurance exists for a period of time, or "term." This can be as short as one year, or longer, like twenty years, or to a definite age like your sixty-fifth birthday. Term insurance was created as a low-cost way to cover a definite need for a specific length of time.

> I have borrowed some money from a friend on a personal note without collateral. The note will be paid back in five years. I agree to protect my friend against the possibility that I might die before repaying the note by taking out a term policy in the amount of the loan for a five-year *term*. When the note is repaid, the need no longer exists so the insurance expires.

Even though the example cites a legitimate use for term insurance, there may still be better ways to provide the protection required.

The second feature that all term plans have in common is that they get increasingly expensive. Whether in 1-year jumps, 5-year increases or 20-year avalanches, term policies go up in cost. Even mortgage-term policies (the face amount decreases along with the mortgage balance, while the premium stays level) must be thought of as going up in cost since the same amount of payment purchases a smaller and smaller amount of coverage.

Ernie and Kay Barton began early in their married life thinking about life insurance. At the time, they could scarcely afford to make the payments on their $25,000 whole-life contract, the absolute minimum in coverage that they felt their young family would need. About 5 years into their premium payments, at a time when Ernie's cash values had reached about $600, the Barton's concluded that they needed to increase the amount of life insurance coverage which they owned, and by that time they could afford to do so.

They were pleased when a friend of theirs indicated that he was a part-time insurance agent and could handle their needs. He suggested that they not bother their previous agent, but look closely at what he had to offer. He excitedly told them that not only could he get them $100,000 of coverage, he could get it for them for no more money than they were paying for the original $25,000 policy. He then proceeded to explain that this was possible because the new policy was term, meaning that it built no cash value. He said the premium would increase as Ernie got older, but that their strategy would be to take the additional money they would have paid for a second-cash-value contract and put that money into an annuity.

The Bartons agreed that this was a good idea and, even though they felt bad about not contacting the previous agent, they surrendered their whole-life policy and took the cash value to use as a deposit in the annuity.

During the 10 years that followed, Ernie and Kay always kept up the life insurance payment, but because the annuity contributions felt more "voluntary" to them, they often skipped that payment. During the early years of the term insurance, the increases in premium were small from year to year. But by the 10th year they began to get larger, so that the cost of the term insurance alone ate up most of what would have been set aside toward the annuity had they been sending it.

Near the end of the 12th-policy year disaster struck. Ernie was found to have a brain tumor which, while operable, affected his speech and partially paralyzed the right side of his body, making him unable to work.

What followed happened in quick succession. First, the Bartons discovered that they did not have a loan provision on the annuity contract, as would have been true with the cash value in the original life insurance policy. Consequently, to get some additional money in the crisis, they had to surrender the annuity contract. Because it had a surrender penalty for the first fifteen years of the contract, they suffered a substantial loss in the interest that their deposits had earned, so they got back little more than a refund of their contributions.

Next, Ernie discovered that when their friend wrote the term-life policy for them, he had failed to include a disability premium waiver, so Ernie and Kay were still responsible for keeping up the life insurance payments even though Ernie was out of work with the prospect of a long-term disability, and even though the life insurance premiums continued to go up with each passing year.

When they examined the contract they discovered that over the next 10 years of premium increases, the payment would be double what they had originally been paying; over the 10 years following that, it would quadruple. Moreover, it was pointless for them to look for cheaper coverage elsewhere, since Ernie, by reason of his medical history, is not at all insurable.

Consequently, the Bartons have seen the meager savings in their annuity wiped out and have already realized that they will not be able to continue payments on the life insurance policy into the period of time when it becomes increasingly likely that Ernie will die and they will very much need the life insurance.

The Bartons have been sorry many times for not taking the simple step of going back to their original life insurance agent and asking his advice before making the change. When their situation was brought to his attention by a mutual acquaintance, he unhappily agreed that there was very little the Bartons could do now to remedy their situation.

Cash Value Insurance

Life insurance policies that build a cash value can be subdivided into two categories that can be labeled "traditional" and "nontraditional."

Traditional Policies

Traditional policies come under a variety of names. They may be referred to as "whole life," "cash value," "permanent," or "paid up." These policies all have certain features in common.

First, they all have a fixed premium that is determined by the age and condition of health at the time the policy was first purchased. This payment is fixed and can never be changed regardless of changes in your health for as long as you own the policy.

Second, all of these policies build cash equity that can be borrowed against, or for which the policy can be surrendered if the coverage is no longer desired.

Third, a traditional policy may be "paid up," meaning that at a certain age, or after a certain number of years there is sufficient cash value for the policy to remain in force with no further premium payments required. All traditional cash-value policies permit an amount of coverage to be frozen with no further payments required, even though the policy does not have enough cash value to "pay up" the entire face amount.

Fourth, as another option to cashing in the policy or taking an amount of paid-up insurance, a third possibility is called "extended term." This means that the cash value is used to keep the full amount of coverage in force, with no further premium payments required for a specified length of time less than being fully paid up.

Fifth, traditional cash-value policies are *initially* more expensive to purchase than an equal amount of term insurance. But while the cash-value policy locks in a premium amount, the payment required for the term plan continues to rise, passing the cost of the cash-value policy and continuing on upward.

Sixth, the cash value accruing in a traditional policy earns tax-deferred interest at a rate guaranteed by their issuing company. In the earlier years of this century, this interest rate was 2 or 3 percent. In recent years it has risen to as much as 5½ or 6 percent.

Seventh, traditional policies may be "participating." This means the issuing company declares a dividend to be returned to the policy holders. The dividend can be taken in cash, or used to purchase additional amounts of life insurance, but is most often added to the cash value where it serves to enhance the accumulation beyond that of the guarantee. "Par plans," as they are called, are somewhat more expensive than "non-par" plans.

Nontraditional Plans

In the early 1980s, the American insurance-buying public was introduced to the concept of nontraditional cash-value products. If you recall, this period was characterized by double-digit inflation, with mortgage rates over 15 percent. An average investor could earn 12 to 14 percent on various types of savings. This situation made the typical insurance buyer reluctant to purchase a life insurance policy still paying a fixed 5-percent return. A certain portion of the insurance industry espoused the position that the correct consumer response should be to buy the least expensive term insurance possible, take the difference in premium savings and invest these dollars at a more competitive rate of return.

This "buy term and invest the difference" philosophy resulted in many traditional-policy holders surrendering their plans and making other arrangements for both their life insurance protection and their cash values.

For a variety of reasons, this has not proved to be a satisfactory solution:

First of all, term insurance has a dismal record of not being in force when needed. Because term insurance gets increasingly expensive as the insured gets older—even prohibitively expensive—many individuals are forced to drop their protection even as their advancing age makes death more likely. The net result of this action is that fewer than 1 out of 10 term-life policies is actually in force at the point of death.

Not only did those insurance buyers throw away their insurance purchasing dollars on a product that gave them no return, but the ever-increasing cost eventually voided the protection that was the original purpose of the purchase.

Second, many people need, and many more *benefit* from the enforced disciplined savings that a cash-value policy provides. The loan provision on cash-value policies make them excellent emergency-fund repositories.

The alternative investments used on the "invest the difference" portion of that advice also suffered from two flaws.

First, these investment alternatives to cash-value buildup seldom performed as well as promised. While 15-percent returns were projected, the reality was often times much lower.

Second, because many investments were not within the tax-sheltered protection of cash-value life insurance, the improved rate of return (if any) was negated by the current taxes being charged on the investment gain.

> When Jess and Melissa Hume were approached by an agent of a company espousing the "buy term and invest the difference" philosophy, they listened to what he had to say because he was a friend. He seemed so enthusiastic, so committed and so sincere that they were shocked to hear him say that companies selling cash-value insurance had nothing but sinister profit motives in mind and actually lied to their policy holders. The friend encouraged them to get the cash value out of their existing policies and make a deposit into a mutual fund—which he said had a wonderful track record, earning 15 to 20 percent a year—and replace their life insurance protection with what he said was the cheapest term insurance you could buy.

> The Humes were startled by all of these revelations. They called their present insurance agent to request cash surrender forms for their life insurance. Since he had always been good to contact them at least once a year, offering to review their coverages, they agreed to let him come to their home and visit with them about the proposed changes.

> The agent who had sold them the cash-value policies pointed out that what they owned were universal life policies, paying a current interest rate of 8½ percent interest, tax deferred. This, he explained, compared very favorably with a 12-percent return on a taxable investment such as a mutual fund. He mentioned that mutual funds, while an

extremely good investment, do not have guarantees and can actually have a negative return (i.e., be worth less than what you paid for them) over any given period of time. He pointed out that the life insurance contract had a 5-percent minimum guaranteed rate and moreover bore a premium that would not be increased as the Humes grew older.

He compared this with the term-life proposal, noting that when the Humes reached age 60, the term-insurance premium that had cost a minimal amount at the beginning would by then cost hundreds of dollars per month! Finally, he said it was not true that companies selling traditional or cash-value products lied to their customers. He demonstrated this by his willingness to go over any and all contract features—things which the other agent said were not important, or could be ignored.

The Humes decided to stay with their cash-value product, even though their friend accused them of being misled. The Humes have since made two further observations about the correctness of their decision. First, their universal life policies accrued so much cash value that they were able to borrow against them to pay for their children's college education—while being charged a mere 4-percent interest for the loan and keeping their life insurance policies in force with the same premium they had been paying for many years. Further, they happened to see in their local paper that some mutual funds had taken a real beating, among them the fund suggested by their salesman friend. The article in the paper noted that $1000 invested in that fund the previous year would then have been worth only $250, and it suggested the fund would take a great many years to recover.

Most insurance companies got creative when they recognized that traditional cash-value products were not designed to compete with double-digit rates of return, and that the "buy term" idea was badly flawed. The result was the creation of nontraditional, cash-value life insurance— programs that combined the best features of both term insurance and traditional cash-value products. Whole-life policies that had locked-in premiums along with a variable and more competitive rate of return were introduced, but the most creative thinking resulted in universal life policies.

The name universal is not intended to sound cosmic or nuclear, even though it has a futuristic ring to it. Instead, the title is intended to refer to the universality of this policy's application to a variety of needs.

A universal life policy has a variable rate of interest, paid by the issuing company in accord with a formula or set of guidelines. Second, a universal plan can have its face amount increased without purchasing an additional policy, or decreased without surrendering all the coverage. Finally, the premium being paid may be increased over the minimum needed to sustain the plan in order to improve the cash value buildup. Or it can be decreased in time of need, letting the cash values present make a portion of the payment for you. This threefold flexibility is what makes the universal policy particularly attractive.

Universal life cash values still receive the tax-deferred treatment of traditional cash-value policies, but earn much better returns. The improved cash-value accumulation, together with the lower cost of these plans, makes them desirable for a great many people.

An Additional Universal-Life Benefit

Traditional policies have been criticized, and justly so, for referring to cash values as belonging to the policy holder. In fact, the company retains those cash values if the insured died.

A $25,000 whole-life policy has $5000 of cash value at the time of the insured's death. The policy pays the beneficiary $25,000 and the insurance company retains the $5000 cash value.

Universal life, and other modern, nontraditional plans, allow the original face amount to function as a minimum death benefit while permitting the accumulating cash values to increase the actual death benefit to be paid.

A $25,000 universal life policy has $5000 of cash value at the time of the insured's death. The beneficiary would receive $30,000 as a death benefit.

Variable Universal Policies

The most recent development of all in the nontraditional product arena is a plan called *variable universal life*. While similar to universal life in many respects, it has the additional feature of allowing the insured to direct the cash value accumulation into any of a number of different investment types. If universal life's cash values can be thought of as being held in a money market fund earning variable but conservative interest, variable universal permits the cash values to be stored in the insured's choice of money market fund, growth-type mutual fund, bond-type mutual fund, even a real estate fund.

The V.U.L. plans have exciting possibilities while still maintaining the tax-deferred quality of the cash values. They will require careful study to determine the appropriateness of the investment choice for each family's situation, and may call for more active review and revision than life insurance has needed before.

Fortunately, all types of universal life plans, whether variable or not, produce an annual report of their performance. This statement gives a detailed accounting of each payment, the resulting investment results, and loan activity or withdrawals from the plan and the projected values in these areas for the next year and several years into the future.

A Word of Caution

Universal life policies should not be entered into lightly. While possessing a minimum guaranteed rate of return, the *current returns* can and do change. The cost of insurance (that is, the dollar cost associated with a certain amount of insurance for a certain age) does increase as you get older. You may never be aware of this increase, since a properly constructed universal life plan takes in more than enough premium payments in the early years of the policy for the cash value to easily sustain the increased costs in later years.

Beware of plans being sold to you on the basis of rock-bottom premiums; these policies will run into trouble later on. Also, beware of unrealistic interest-rate projections. Two percent better than inflation makes for a good conservative projection; and the phrase, "no more than 6 percent better than the current inflation rate," will help you judge even the most optimistic proposal.

Exercising correct judgment and proper review should not mean that you must shy away from universal life plans. Treat them as you would a new automobile: Given careful attention and occasional tune-ups, they will deliver high performance and years of satisfaction.

> When Kermit Neilson met Rae, whom he later married, he already owned a $50,000 universal life insurance policy. He had liked the level-premium payment and the tax-deferred savings feature. At the time he took out the policy, he had no dependents and little debt, but he was smart enough to realize that by locking in the premium payment at his young age, he could look forward to modestly priced protection and substantial cash-value build up.

> When he and Rae decided to purchase a home, they were offered mortgage-cancelation insurance through the lending institution. But before agreeing to take it out, they called to ask my opinion. I suggested they examine the possibility of increasing Kermit's existing life insurance policy by the amount of the mortgage note, since this would give them the additional protection needed to pay off the mortgage. Rae asked if this would not eventually be too much insurance, since the mortgage balance would decline with time while the life insurance face amount would not automatically reduce. We visited about this point for some time.

> The Neilsons concluded that their standard of living would certainly increase as time went by. Moreover, if Kermit should die Rae would certainly benefit from the additional life insurance, even if the lump sum were not entirely required to pay off the mortgage. In addition, I pointed out that the additional cash-value buildup would give them something to look forward to.

> We also discussed the advisability of taking out a universal

life policy on Rae since her wages were also being used in part to support the home mortgage payment.

Years later when Rae was no longer working, she had still kept up the payments on her life insurance policy and her cash values had amounted to quite a tidy sum. Since the Neilsons did not feel a need to continue her life insurance protection (she was no longer working and their children were grown), they cashed in Rae's policy and used the money to pay their mortgage balance off seven years early. This action saved the Neilsons an additional $14,000 in interest charges they would have paid had they continued the mortgage to its 30-year conclusion.

A Comparison of Term, Whole Life, and Universal Life

Term Life Insurance
1. Low initial cost.
2. Increasing cost (or decreasing benefit).
3. May expire, has no cash equity.

Whole Life Insurance
1. Higher initial cost.
2. Level lifetime cost.
3. Level lifetime protection.
4. Tax-favored cash reserve buildup.

Universal Life Insurance
1. Moderate initial cost.
2. Flexible premium.
3. Adjustable death benefit.
4. Competitive interest on tax-favored cash reserves.
5. Policy pays off face-amount, plus cash values at death.

Reviewing My Personal Situation:
Life Insurance Types

1. I presently own (circle one):
   a. Term life insurance.
   b. Cash-value insurance.
   c. Some of each.
   d. Not sure.
2. My term life insurance policies (circle one):
   a. Go down in death benefit.
   b. Go up in price.
   c. Some of each.
   d. Not sure.
3. My cash value policies have (circle one):
   a. A fixed rate-of-return.
   b. A variable rate-of-return.
   c. Some of each.
   d. Not sure.
4. I'm presently paying $＿＿＿＿＿＿ for my life insurance protection. And my total death benefit is $＿＿＿＿＿＿ .
5. I am (circle one):
   a. Satisfied with my present plan.
   b. Unsatisfied with my present plan.
   c. Unclear and need more information.
6. I am (circle one):
   a. Comfortable talking to the agent who sold me my policy.
   b. Uncomfortable talking to the agent who sold me my policy.
   c. Prefer to talk to someone *in addition* to the agent.

10

Life Insurance: How Much Is Enough?

LIFE INSURANCE serves the dual purpose of protecting a family's financial security *and* providing a safe and effective storage location for emergency funds. As we have seen, modern life insurance policies are much more than just death protection. They can be valuable financial instruments and serve as the foundation of a family's financial planning. This double purpose makes life insurance the perfect jumping-off point from which to leave our consideration of risk management and turn to the subject of investment management. Before we do, however, some attention must be devoted to the unpleasant but necessary question, "How much life insurance is enough?"

We are instructed in Prov. 13:22:

A good man leaves an inheritance for his children's children.

Russ and Nola Hyatt "realized" that life insurance was a bad investment. Moreover, they thought the whole subject so unpleasant they found it easier to put off the discussion of it.

The insurance agent who insured their home attempted to bring up the subject on a couple of occasions, but the Hyatts had a built-in excuse. They found could end the conversation by saying, "Russ has adequate protection at work." In their minds they sincerely believed this to be true, since Russ's group benefits at his employment included a $100,000 term life policy. Though they had never sat down to add up the amount that would be needed if Russ died, they felt certain that the $100,000, together with the $10,000 they had in savings, would be more than enough.

Nola will never have the chance to know for certain whether their reasoning was correct, because when Russ died he had only recently changed jobs. He had made the change because it gave him a 25-percent increase in salary and he never even asked what the benefit package included. Even if he had asked, it is doubtful that the meager life-insurance benefit of $5000 would have kept him from making the change. Consequently, when he died, Nola's protection totaled only $15,000, since they had kept about the same $10,000 in their emergency savings and spent most of the rest.

When it came time to add up the obligations, Nola found the following to be true: Just the funeral arrangements took the $5000 coverage that Russ had from work, and the $10,000 savings disappeared rather rapidly in final medical bills and legal fees. Since their home was not paid for and the remaining mortgage balance was some $50,000, Nola's salary was not adequate to cover both the mortgage payment and the upkeep of the home. Russ and Nola's children were grown, and she had not yet reached Social Security eligibility and was in the so-called "black-out period," so she received no government benefits.

Nola was forced to sell her home and move into an apartment. She is now a lay counselor in her church's family financial guidance workshop, and she never misses an opportunity to counsel couples to thoroughly investigate and understand their life insurance needs.

Incorrect Methods of Deciding on Amount of Coverage

Some people feel that determining life insurance protection is someone else's job. By this, they may mean that they purchase whatever amount the agent suggests, without justification. They may also mean that their life insurance protection is whatever their employment benefits provide; if $25,000, well, then okay; if only $10,000, that must be right, too.

Some insurance buyers feel the need to select the amount personally, but do so based on some formula that they believe was suggested. (Four times your annual income—or was that supposed to be six times?) Still others choose a level of coverage based on what "sounds right"; doesn't $100,000 sound like a good round number? What method did you use in arriving at your protection amount, and when did you review it last?

We need to get an understanding of how you can make an informed choice of amount, and to do this we must first examine what life insurance protection is supposed to accomplish.

Cash Needs at Death

Some people regard life insurance as synonymous with burial expenses. While the cost of funerals is certainly an item to be included in an examination of cash needs at death, it is by no means the only item.

Cash needs at death actually include a variety of debts and obligations that would be best to have satisfied at the time of the wage earner's death. The first subheading can be called final expenses.

Final Expenses

These include funeral costs, legal fees and outstanding medical bills. I am often asked to estimate the cost of funerals and I can only give a range at best. Funeral expenses can cost anywhere from $3000 for a simple ceremony, and up. Most people find that a figure of around $5000 is realistic. I encourage you to do some "pre-need" investigation into this unpleasant but necessary subject; grief-stricken families are notoriously unable to cope with financial decisions in the immediacy of their feelings of loss.

> A client of mine, the pastor of a small church, lost his wife of 40 years. In the midst of his sorrow, he also suffered the indignity of having to borrow $3000 to pay for her funeral. This was, he confided to me in a tearful and broken voice, despite the fact that her service was held in his own church and he bought only the plainest "pine box" and a modest cemetery plot.

Legal fees depend on the complexity of the estate to be settled and the number of transactions involved. The costs in this area can be kept down by having a current will and keeping it updated. The subject of wills is so important that we'll devote an entire chapter to it elsewhere. A reasonable allowance for the legal fee category might be about $5000.

> A friend of mine whose grandmother passed away was in charge of the arrangements. Even though the estate consisted of $50,000 in certificates of deposit and no other assets, the attorney fees came to 10 percent, or $5000.

Remaining medical costs will depend on how much out-of-pocket cost is allowed by the health-care plan. Obviously, the figure can mushroom in the absence of good health insurance, since illnesses resulting in death can often be lengthy and costly. Without specific knowledge of your present medical coverage, let's estimate another $5000 as being (hopefully) adequate.

The total, then, of estimated final expenses—which is just the first topic in our study of cash needs at death—comes to $15,000.

Mortgage Cancelation

Most folks agree that the necessity of protecting their home against foreclosure because of the untimely death of the wage earner is of primary importance. Since home mortgages nowadays commonly reach figures of $80,000 to $100,000 or more, you can see that this, by itself, would make for life insurance needs far in excess of what your group coverage at work probably allows.

Some lending institutions will offer you a mortgage cancelation coverage, with the added convenience of having the premium added to your mortgage payment. There are three reasons why it is probably *not* in your best interest to protect your mortgage in this way.

First, this form of life insurance is relatively expensive. Cheaper forms of mortgage protection are available as individual life insurance policies.

Second, such coverage is a decreasing form of insurance, designed to decline in value as the mortgage balance declines. Hence, what you started out paying for becomes more and more expensive as *the amount of value* for your payment *declines while your payment remains the same*. Additionally, since many families purchase more than one home, with new (and often higher) mortgage balances, the amount of premiums paid would have been wasted as the homeowner must begin a new program of protection at a higher cost due to increased age.

Finally, such coverage pays only the lending institution in the event of the insured's death. While this is exactly what the policy is designed to do, it does not permit the survivors the option of making that decision for themselves. In some situations, it may be advantageous to continue making the payments and use the life insurance proceeds as income.

> Clay and Glenda Lee were extremely proud of their home when they purchased it, because it had taken them such a long time to save up the down payment and to find exactly the right home in exactly the right neighborhood.
>
> Clay discussed with Glenda the importance of making sure that the home was adequately protected against his untimely death, since he was the sole wage earner in the family. Glenda agreed, and so both of them were pleased when the lending institution handling their home mortgage offered them "mortgage-cancelation insurance" that would pay off their $65,000 balance if Clay should die. The $30 premium could even be paid with their monthly mortgage deposit.
>
> Over the next several years, the Lees were approached on

a few occasions by life insurance agents who suggested that what they were paying for home mortgage protection was higher in cost than what they could obtain the coverage for elsewhere. Or that, in any case, the Lees should review their life insurance protection to cover other necessities at the time of death.

Clay and Glenda realized that they had not purchased the least expensive life insurance protection. They also realized that it was getting more expensive as Clay grew older, because it only promised to pay off the mortgage balance. Hence, the same $30 payment that they paid month in and month out with their mortgage check was purchasing a smaller and smaller amount of protection. They reasoned, however, that their payment was accomplishing exactly what they intended it to do—namely, guaranteeing that Glenda would have a debt-free home in the event that Clay died without having completed paying off the mortgage. So they decided to let matters remain as they were. They also felt that, since their home was their most substantial debt, they had adequately protected their family in the way of life insurance. (This is an example of how a little bit of protection becomes a "conscience vaccination" that prevents a family from getting concerned enough about an issue to do what they really need to do.)

In the 20th year of the 30-year mortgage, Clay did in fact die tragically of an infection that turned to blood poisoning. After the funeral, Glenda took stock of her financial situation. She was comforted when the bank presented her a mortgage statement showing that their balance was paid in full and the deed to her home was now free and clear. Since the Lees had no other life insurance and very little savings, Glenda decided that the best thing she could do under the circumstances was to sell the home. Unfortunately, the neighborhood which they had found so attractive 20 years earlier was now not as popular as it once had been. Worse yet, Clay had died during a time of double-digit home mortgage rates, so prospective buyers asked Glenda to take rather large reductions in the asking price of the home. Since she correctly felt that this was like giving up her only savings, Glenda decided to try to refinance the home and use the money to open a small gift shop which she reasoned could support her and make the home's mortgage payment as well.

However, the same lending institution that had always handled their home mortgage startled Glenda. First, the size of the monthly payment she was quoted was huge. (Remember, the refinance loan came at a higher rate of interest than the first loan.) Second, they denied her the loan anyway. The bank realized that the property was not as desirable now as it had been, that it would be difficult to sell in the event of a foreclosure, and Glenda had no track record to prove her ability to operate a business.

Ultimately, Glenda sold the home for $20,000 less than what she had originally anticipated getting. She has since moved in with a sister in another state and is using the interest from her remaining savings to pay her sister for her room and board while she goes to night school. At 50 years of age, Glenda knows that without some further education she will never be offered anything other than minimum-wage employment.

Other Debts

Other cash needs at death could include car loans, credit card debts and other financial notes or obligations. Most people agree that it would be best for a family just beginning to put their life back together after the loss of a loved one in a debt-free environment. The same reasoning as was used in our discussion of mortgage-cancelation insurance applies to the credit-life coverages that are often available with loans.

Children's Fund

Often called an "education" or "vocation" fund, this category of cash needs suggests that you set aside the sum of money which you would have used to launch your children into college or a career. Families will need to discuss seriously whether they wish to undertake this obligation at all and, if so, what financial provision is anticipated. There can be a tremendous variety of estimates for this area, ranging from zero to $100,000.

Miscellaneous

An emergency fund asks a family to explore how much should be set aside to meet unexpected expenses, much the same as if the wage earner were still living. This category includes such things as car repairs, replacement of broken appliances, and unexpected dental or medical bills. The estimate difficulty is compounded somewhat because of the need to allow for those services or repairs that would have been performed by the wage earner. Estimates range from as low as $5000 to as much as 6-month's income. An average figure for this need seems to be $10,000.

Summarizing Cash Needs at Death

The amount of protection needed for cash needs at death is derived by adding up the five categories: final expenses, mortgage cancelation, other debts, children's fund and miscellaneous. The actual amount required for your family will depend on your own situation and how conscientiously you estimate the various areas.

These figures are not set in stone, and should be reevaluated and revised as needed once a year.

The Evans family finds a total of $75,000 in cash needs. This represents the sum of $20,000 in final expenses, $15,000 in remaining home mortgage balance, $10,000 in car and credit card debt, $10,000 to assist their youngest son in school, and $20,000 in an emergency fund.

The Moores find $20,000 to be adequate. This number is arrived at by adding $5000 for final expenses, $7000 each for car loans and emergency fund and $1000 in "seed" money for their 6-month-old baby. They are not purchasing a home at this time.

The MacDonalds combine an $80,000 mortgage payoff with $10,000 each in final expenses, debts, and emergency fund for a total in cash needs of $110,000.

Family Income Needs

In determining how much coverage is enough, the second half of the life insurance equation results from the question of family income need. What amount of monthly income is required for your present monthly expenses? How much less than your current budget could your family live on if you were not around? How much of this amount would be available to them and from what sources? How much would have to come from new sources?

These and similar questions go into determining the family income need.

What Resources Are Already Available?

After the cash needs have been eliminated, there may or may not be some savings left. If there are remaining savings, this amount can be used to provide monthly income. The insurance company may make available a monthly withdrawal plan, paying out so much per month, while continuing to pay interest on the balance. The family may wish to make other arrangements, such as an annuity contract with a guaranteed monthly payout. (See page 156ff.)

Many people think of Social Security as a source of monthly income for widows and orphans. This is correct because Social Security does provide extremely valuable survivor benefits. These benefits depend upon earnings, age and the number of children still living at home. It is important to know what level of benefits your family would be entitled to receive from Social Security, so an appendix dealing with this subject is included in this book. Most important to remember is that there is no Social Security benefit to surviving widows *unless* there are still school-age children living at home. This so-called "black out" period is a key factor to remember in making long-range plans.

Some people feel that a substitute family income could come from the surviving widow reentering the work force. This issue raises the unpleasant concept that many widows do not have marketable skills because they have been out of the work force. Moreover, many widows find that the minimum-wage positions open to them generate as much in increased child care costs as is gained through working.

Some families assume that a necessary response to the loss of a partner would be reduced expectations, or getting along on less. In fact, there would be some reduced costs in food and clothing, but the larger family expenses—like housing and utilities—would not change. As we have mentioned before, any savings in this area would probably be offset by the increased expense of having to hire someone to do the routine repair and maintenance functions previously performed by the now-absent mate.

How Can Life Insurance Produce Monthly Income?

Any amount (or source) of capital can be used to produce income. The simplest illustration of this is the idea of leaving a savings account sum intact, while drawing off the interest for expenses:

> A 10,000 savings account earning 6-percent interest produces $600 a year in interest income. Dividing the $600 into 12 monthly payments would produce a monthly income of $50, leaving the $10,000 balance untouched.

After the cash needs at death have been satisfied, the remaining life insurance proceeds can be used to produce monthly income in just this way.

Estimating Needed Life Insurance: The Capitalization Method

Since we know that life insurance can produce monthly income, it follows that the reverse is also true: If we know how much income is needed per month and what rate of interest can be earned, we can calculate how much life insurance (or other savings) is needed to produce this amount.

> The Jordan family estimates that with their present savings and insurance, the cash needs at death would be eliminated, but with nothing left over.

> After subtracting the expected Social Security benefit, they conclude that their family would still be $1000 per month short of its desired standard of living.

> Since they feel they could earn an 8-percent rate of return safely and conservatively, the calculation then works as follows: $1000 needed each month times 12 months equals $12,000 needed each year; $12,000 divided by .08 (8 percent) equals $150,000.

This means that if the Jordans have $150,000 in any savings (whether from life insurance or some other source), which brought in an 8-percent return, they would receive $1000 per month in income without ever disturbing the $150,000 balance.

Things to Remember in Doing the Calculation

Allow for the immediate, or cash needs first. If you elect to pay off the mortgage balance on your home, this may require a larger cash sum, but should reduce the amount needed in per-month income.

> Rudy and Carmen Garcia own a rental home. It is paid for and worth about $60,000 if sold. It has a good tenant now and a good expectation of remaining occupied. It produces $500 per month in rental income.
>
> Since this property is both savings ($60,000), and income ($500 per month), they will need to discuss how to use it if something happens to Rudy. Remember, it can serve one need, but not both.
>
> They decide it would be best to keep. Using 8 percent as a reasonable investment return, they discover that $60,000 times 8 percent divided into 12 months yields only $400 per month. The Garcias purchase a $60,000 insurance policy instead to settle the cash needs.

Don't overlook either expected expenses or untapped resources in doing your homework. Find out, for instance, if your family can receive part of your employment pension plan as a death benefit and how much this is worth. Don't be extravagant in estimating what your investments will bring in; don't be unrealistic in figuring how much of a reduction from your present budget your family can survive.

> As a young couple, the Shepherds did not feel a particular need for life insurance. Since they had no children and both of them were working and did not own a home, they didn't feel much need for life insurance protection beyond their group employment benefits. They were concerned enough about the subject after they purchased their first home—

and their family had grown to include a two-year-old boy and an infant daughter—that they listened intently when an insurance agent brought up the subject. He suggested they take stock of their present situation by examining first the cash needs that Robin would experience if Stan died.

The Shepherds estimated $5000 for funeral costs and other final expenses, another $5000 for an emergency fund, $50,000 to pay off their home mortgage and another $10,000 as an amount they would like to see available for their children's future educational plans. This total—$70,000—exceeded by $45,000 the amount of protection Stan had at work.

The agent explained that they should also look at the monthly income needs that Robin would face, taking into account available Social Security benefits. Due to the age of the children, however, Robin probably would not be able to work much, nor would this necessarily be desirable, since a large part of her earnings would go out immediately in child-care payments. The capitalized monthly income needs for the Shepherd family came to $150,000, for a total need of close to $200,000.

Since the Shepherds felt they could afford only $50 a month for life insurance, the agent suggested that they take care of the $200,000 need with a combination of cash-value and term insurance, while planning to convert the term insurance to additional cash-value insurance as their budget would allow.

The Shepherds are not only relaxed and confident in the family's financial security, but look forward to their agent's annual visit to review their coverage as a pleasant necessity rather than an unpleasant chore.

What About Life Insurance for Wives and Children?

While there is little argument about the necessity of life insurance protection on the life of the family wage earner, there is some debate about its use for other family members.

Remember that life insurance is designed to aid in sparing the family economic harm in time of death. It is also capable of other benefits because of its current attractive interest rates and tax-favored treatment.

The duties of a wife and mother have more economic value than some families realize. Remember, guys, wives are cooks, seamstresses, housekeepers, chauffeurs, baby-sitters, secretaries, bookkeepers and much, much more! The estimated value of a "domestic engineer's" services range from a low of $18,000 to $30,000 per year or more. Does this sound like an "investment" worth protecting? Moreover, how many families have working mothers? Be honest: Is this second income all surplus, or does part of it go for regular monthly expenses? Could the family get along without it, or would it have to be replaced?

Children's life insurance is a different matter, since they are not often expected to contribute to the family's economic well-being.

This does not mean that there are no valid reasons for children to own life insurance, however. There are two extremely good purposes for a child to have a life insurance policy.

First, insurance on the life of a child acts as a place holder, guaranteeing that child will be able to own life insurance when he or she has a family. Children's policies can even be equipped with the guaranteed right to purchase additional coverage at future dates, even if the child's health will not otherwise permit it.

Second, a child's life insurance policy can be an excellent source of savings. Given the policy's competitive returns and its tax-deferred treatment, a policy on a child is a good place to sock away funds to be used for future plans like college.

Concluding Thoughts

Life insurance policies have gone far beyond death protection, becoming valuable investments. They cannot perform their function properly, though, unless both the type and amount of coverage are selected with great care.

Life insurance cannot replace a loved one. However, it can make the transition into a new phase of a family's life much easier if the policy is sufficient to do the job. This amount can be determined after prayerful consideration and a thorough investigation of your family's life insurance needs.

How many people will not live another 20 years?[1]

The chances of dying within 20 years are:

Age	Male	Female
25	1 in 20	1 in 27
30	1 in 15	1 in 19
35	1 in 10	1 in 14
40	1 in 7	1 in 10
45	1 in 5	1 in 7

Reviewing My Personal Situation:
Life Insurance Needs

1. I presently have $_____ total life insurance protection. These policies cost me $_____ per month. They are term/cash-value/some of each.
2. My family would experience the following cash needs at my death:
   a. Final expenses: _____
   b. Mortgage cancelation: _____
   c. Other debts: _____
   d. Emergency fund: _____
   e. Education/vocation fund: _____
   f. Total: _____
3. To offset the cash needs at my death, my family would have:
   a. Present life insurance: _____
   b. Savings: _____
   c. Other investments: _____
   d. Total: _____

---

[1] 1980 CSO table.

4. My family's monthly income needs would probably be
   $_____ per month.
5. To offset their monthly income needs my family would
   have:
   a. Working spouse (net monthly): _____
   b. Social Security: _____
   c. Other monthly: _____
   d. Total: _____
6. Subtracting the total from question 3 from the total of
   question 2 leaves $_____ of remaining cash needs.
7. A reasonable long-term investment return is _____
   percent (use 8 percent as example).
8. Subtract the total from question 5 from the amount in
   question 4. Multiply this amount by 12; divide it by your
   chosen investment return percent (.08 is our example).
9. Add the results of question 6 and the results of question
   8 to obtain the total remaining insurance needs at death.

PART THREE
INVESTMENT MANAGEMENT

11

Investment Basics

RISK MANAGEMENT has to do with protecting those things that you already have, while investment management goes into the less certain area of how to best *develop* the blessings with which you've been entrusted.

Investment management can be broken down into three goals or objectives. Just like risk management, it has four hazards to be avoided.

The goals for investment management are:

1. Short-term savings
2. Long-term investments
3. Retirement planning

The four things that put accumulation at risk are:

1. Time
2. Inflation
3. Taxes
4. Investment choice

Let's examine the four potential hazards first.

Time

When I list time as a potential hazard to investment success, I'm referring to the fact that different investments require differing amounts of time to operate correctly.

Proper investment management requires that you match up the amount of time needed for the chosen investment to operate with the length of time actually available.

Some types of financial decisions are not affected by time. Savings accounts, for example, and other guaranteed returns will provide the same results whether short term, long term or for retirement. This does not mean that such savings are appropriate for all three uses, as we'll see a little later.

The effect of time is readily apparent on some investments in the form of early withdrawal penalties. Participation in an annuity, for example, requires advance preparation to leave untouched the contents of the contract until the penalty period has elapsed or suffer the consequences. As you can see, the presence of a penalty does not mean that an investment is bad, but merely requires greater advance planning. Similarly, the absence of a penalty does not automatically mean that a particular investment is good for every use.

Finally, some investments may have no penalty for early withdrawal as such, but may innately require more time to succeed. Any account that has an up-front cost to acquire, such as a front-load mutual fund, will immediately be worth less than it cost to purchase. This means that before the investment begins to show any gain, it must first have sufficient growing time to make up the original cost.

Inflation

The rate of inflation is a measure of how prices increase from year to year. Put another way, inflation reflects how much a dollar's purchasing power declines as time goes by.

A turn-of-the-century cartoon titled "When a dollar was a dollar" shows a young boy standing by the counter of a general store and reading from a list, saying:

". . . and a pound of salt, and a pound of coffee, and five pounds of sugar and ten pounds of flour, a dozen eggs, a sack of potatoes and a box of crackers and Mom says I can spend the rest of the dollar on licorice and jelly beans. . . ."

If this sounds farfetched, how long ago was gasoline less than a dollar a gallon? How about the 25-cent hamburger? When my wife and I purchased our first home, we paid $17,000 for it. Our second home, which was brand new and some 1500 square feet in size, was only $30,000. (And we're talking about the early 1970s, not the 1900s!)

Supply and demand, rising labor costs, oil embargoes—all of these factors combine to drive up prices worldwide. Aren't you glad that we're not concerned here with trying to understand and explain inflation? What we want to be able to do is *cope* with it, because it is a real hazard to investment success.

The hazard posed by inflation is this: Suppose that prices are increasing at 10 percent per year. This means that it takes $1.10 of my hard-earned money to purchase next year what $1 would purchase this year. If during that same year a dollar that I've committed to savings only increases by 6-percent interest, I only have $1.06 to buy what now costs $1.10.

Now it is not possible for all investments to beat inflation. Nor can we say with confidence that inflation will never be a problem again. Nonetheless, there are ways to stand up to inflation and win!

Taxes

The third potential hazard addressed by investment management is taxes. Jesus said, "Give to Caesar what is Caesar's, and to God what is God's." Our concern is how to avoid giving Caesar too much of what is God's—or ours either, for that matter!

Each year a substantial part of our earnings is paid to federal and state governments in the form of income taxes. What many fail to consider is the effect income taxes have on investment earnings. You see, most dollars saved in this country are in investments subject to taxation. Put another way, not only are the dollars we earn taxed, but the interest dollars our dollars earn are taxed, too.

The federal income tax rate structure contains only two brackets: 15 percent and 28 percent. This means that after subtracting allowable deductions and exemptions, what remains as taxable income will be subject to taxes in one of two percentages. The bracket into which your income will fall depends on your earnings and your filing status (single, married/filing jointly, etc.). The hazard to investment success posed here is that interest earnings count as income and have to be included in the total income figure.

> A family in the 15-percent income tax bracket earns $100 in interest on a savings account.

> Since that $100 is counted as income, after paying Uncle Sam his share the family will get to keep $85.

What's more, the state in which you live may subject your income (and therefore your non-tax qualified investments) to a state income tax. This can be a significant additional loss of earnings, since the various state income tax rates range upward to as high as 13½ percent of taxable income.

> A family living in a state with a 10-percent state income tax and who are in the 28-percent bracket for federal income tax will get to keep $620 of $1000 of investment gain.

Knowing my tax bracket allows me to determine ahead of time what the effect of income taxes will be on the interest I earn. Whatever interest rate an investment earns must be reduced by the tax-bracket percentage.

> A credit union account paying 6-percent interest is fully subject to income taxation.

> If my bracket is determined to be 28 percent, then my credit union earnings will actually be 4.32 percent.

> An easy way to do this calculation is to say, what percentage of income do I get to keep? In this case, $100 - 28 = 72$ percent after taxes. We then multiply that figure times the interest rate promised: 72 percent $\times$ 6 = 4.32 percent.

Finally, knowing in advance the taxation which my interest earnings will be subject to helps me plan ways to allow for that reduction.

The Murphy family has a $10,000 inheritance to invest. They would like to earn at least $750 in interest.

Their tax advisor suggests that they will be in the 15-percent bracket.

You can see that they must receive 7.5 percent in interest net (after taxes) ($750 divided by $10,000 = 7.5 percent).

Now the question they need to ask is, "Since we will get to keep 85 percent of what we make (100 − 15 = 85) what interest rate is required to still leave 7.5 percent after taxes?"

The answer to this question is found by dividing 7.5 by 85 percent (7.5 divided by .85): The result is 8.8 percent.

The Murphy family will actually receive $750 in interest to spend (all taxes paid) if they invest their $10,000 in something that pays at least 8.8 percent.

As you can see, taxation requires a good deal of advance planning and prayer for us to be successful investment managers.

Ralph and Mildred are proud of their investment ability. They have concluded that CD's (certificates of deposit) are just right for them because they want safety and a better return than on passbook savings.

The current rate of return on their CD's is 7 percent. Since they are in the 28-percent income tax bracket, they will actually get to keep 72 percent of their earned interest or 5.04 percent (7 × .72 = 5.04 percent).

Given the historical fact that inflation averages 6 percent per year, each year that they invest at 7 percent and pay taxes in the 28-percent bracket, they go about 1 percent in the hole (5.04 − 6 = -.96).

Are they wrong to believe in CD's? Not necessarily. The reasoning about safety is sound, and even after taxes, the CD's are doing a better job of keeping up with inflation than passbook savings would.

Could they do even better? Possibly, but they will need to do further study.

Investment Choice

The fourth and final potential hazard is the investment choice. It should be apparent to you from the number of people and institutions vying for your attention on precisely this point that this subject alone could fill several more volumes.

Since I promised early on in this book that our discussion of financial planning would not "push" any school of economic thought or investment strategy, we will deal only with some common sense guidelines for investing. We'll try to point out some of the factors that need to be considered, and then trust that a thorough study of your personal situation will lead you further.

Inappropriate Choice

I mentioned before that there are three realms of investment planning: short term, long term, and retirement. Into the areas you are considering must be injected an analysis of the three potential hazards already referred to: time, inflation and taxes.

Are you familiar with the word *optimum* as it relates to investment? It means the best choice for the circumstances. It would be nice if there existed an investment that was free of income tax, always out-performed inflation and had absolutely no risk, while returning such magnificent results in no time at all. *Dream on!* Since no such investment exists, we will have to content ourselves with making some "optimum" choices.

Liquidity

Liquidity refers to the ease with which an investment can be "tapped," or converted to cash. Liquidity is not a hazard to investment except as it may determine the appropriateness of a choice. Passbook savings are extremely liquid; the funds, both principal and interest, are available to be withdrawn on any banking day. Even more liquid would be an interest-bearing checking account, since you needn't even go to the bank to use the funds. Some non-liquid investments, real estate for example, would be appropriate for long-term investing, but not for short term. Extremely liquid investments generally provide a lower rate of return than less liquid choices.

Bad Advice, Lack of Personal Knowledge

A large factor contributing to inappropriate investment choice is basing your decision on the incorrect advice of others. The incorrectness may result from a lack of expertise on the part of the advisor, or it may come from the advisor's desire to slant you toward a particular product. (See Appendix B.)

The best defense against bad advice is to have a personal knowledge of the institution or program in which you've chosen to invest. The reference section of your public library will contain many helpful works for your study, including the volumes of various independent rating services. Larger libraries will even provide the services of a reference librarian to assist you in getting started. As you become more acquainted with different investment choices, you will want to review the many consumer and investment periodicals, weighing their advice against your own experience.

Diversity

The final factor in our discussion of appropriate investment choice is a simple one: "Don't put all your eggs in one basket." It is not possible for one program to meet all your needs; it is probably not possible for one institution to hold the key to all your investment requirements.

Don't expect, just on the basis of reading this book, to be able to resolve all your questions for the remainder of your financial lives. Let's make it a goal to start acquiring the basic skills, knowledge and confidence to begin assembling a portfolio. Don't let the word portfolio scare you, it just means that diversity which enables you to balance poor with better results, and unfortunate choices with inspired ones.

Concluding Thoughts

Just as there are four potential hazards to income, so there are four potential hazards or risks to be avoided in successful investment management. These are the effect of time on investments, the importance of allowing for inflation when making investment decisions, the effect of taxation on savings and the necessity of making an appropriate choice for your deposit.

Making an appropriate choice for your needs depends upon whether the savings is intended for short term, long term or for retirement. In addition, the factors to be considered when judging appropriateness are liquidity, personal knowledge and diversity.

12

Investment Choices

As WE NOTED in the last chapter, juggling the many factors that affect successful investing depends in part on having a clear picture as to the use for any particular deposit. What is appropriate for a short-term savings plan would not be correct for a longer term program.

What we will attempt to do in this chapter is to examine briefly the concerns that should be addressed in your planning for each of the three investment lengths. We'll also try to make some general suggestions as to what investments others have found to be appropriate for different uses. I need to stress again that it is not possible to make such generic advice answer specific questions. My purpose is to alert you to problems and potential solutions.

Short Term Versus "Put-and-Take"

Passbook Savings

Before we examine the kinds of questions faced by those arranging their short-term savings, we must first come to an agreement about what that phrase means. You can distinguish between short-term savings and "put-and-take" savings. The latter refers to where you keep money to pay current or expected expenses.

Some people feel that they have short-term savings because they keep their household budget in a passbook savings account. This is commendable because of the safety provided (insured to $100,000 by the Federal Deposit Insurance Corporation—FDIC) and because you can earn some interest on the deposits; but it does *not* qualify as savings. As we have seen, passbook savings accounts are terribly abused by both taxes and inflation. Consequently, it is best to keep only the month's budget amount in passbook savings, or its more recent counterpart, the interest-bearing checking account. Neither is a satisfactory location for more than one month's funds.

Credit Union Accounts

The other need met by "put-and-take" savings besides safety is *liquidity*. Liquidity, you recall, is the availability of funds on demand. While passbook savings and checking accounts certainly answer this need, there are better options possible. One that comes immediately to mind is the credit union account. If you are eligible to participate in one, you will find that it pays a slightly better return than conventional savings while maintaining perfect safety.

Many credit unions will now allow checks to be written on credit union deposit accounts (called "share drafts"), therefore allowing members much the same freedom as banks. The credit union arrangement functions somewhat better than bank accounts, but not enough better to qualify as short-term savings.

Money Market Funds

Still in the category of "put-and-take" programs are money market funds. A money market fund is a pool of invested dollars that the investment firm uses to purchase monetary instruments, such as certificates of deposit, treasury-sheltering bills and other federal government obligations.

Money market funds, while not insured, generally invest in guaranteed programs and therefore share this level of safety with their participants. Because the pool of invested funds is large enough to purchase denominations of investments whose minimums would be beyond the reach of most individual savers, they can obtain a better return than either passbook savings or credit union accounts.

Money market funds often have a minimum initial investment, but in recent years this has declined to as little as $100, making the eligibility to participate almost universal. Additionally, most money market funds now offer a check writing privilege, thus making the funds perfectly liquid as well. Money market funds cannot replace local accounts completely since check writing is usually restricted to a certain minimum amount ($500, for instance).

This combination of safety, liquidity and a slightly better return make money market funds an ideal location for the emergency fund we've referred to before. In fact, the first order of business in putting your investment-management house in order is the accumulation of a minimum of three months' income; six months' is even better. After this goal has been reached, funds accumulating in the money market fund can be withdrawn by check in order to make deposits in other investments as they are selected.

Short-Term Savings

Let's define what short-term savings actually means.

Short-term savings can be thought of as those deposits made for five years or less. Short-term savings still exhibit a high degree of safety, but cope with inflation and taxes by staying even (at least) in purchasing power. "Put-and-take" plans cannot keep pace with inflation because of their dependence on the issuing financial institutions. Since banks, credit unions and money market funds invest their deposits in places that are only a few percent ahead of inflation, it follows that once this "middle-man" activity is deducted, the resulting interest to the individual saver will be minimal at best.

Good short-term programs are often thought to include: time savings certificates, treasury bills and certificates of deposit.

Time Savings Certificates

A time savings certificate is a financial instrument issued by a bank that requires a minimum deposit (from as little as $500 to as much as $50,000). The deposit is made for a specified period of time, which may be a period of weeks to as long as several years.

There are substantial penalties for withdrawing the funds before their maturity date, but this reduced liquidity is compensated for by a higher rate of interest.

Time savings certificates offer complete safety, but the interest earned is fully taxable. Sometimes a good strategy would include time savings deposits made in a child's name in order to reduce or eliminate the income tax liability. Recent tax law changes have made it imperative that investments made in a child's name be monitored carefully; interest income above a certain level is taxed at the parent's rate.

Incidentally, tax law and its subsequent interpretation by the courts has shown that, while it is the duty of every citizen to pay his or her tax obligation, it is equally proper to use all legal means to avoid paying more than necessary. Thus there is no legal or ethical barrier to proper tax sheltering.

Treasury Bills

Treasury bills are a popular form of short-term investment. They generally mature in one year or less, but are tied up for that period of time.

T-bills are sold at a discount, meaning you pay less than their face amount to acquire them, and the interest they earn matures them up to the face amount. However, T-bills are not available to savers trying to set aside small monthly sums, as they usually have a $10,000 minimum. The income is subject to income tax when the bill matures.

A good strategy to use if T-bills are of interest to you is to make regular deposits into a money market fund until the T-bill minimum is met. (Remember to leave untouched the family emergency fund!)

Certificates of Deposit

Certificates of deposit pay competitive rates of interest since the investor is loaning substantial sums of money to the issuing bank ($10,000 to $100,000). There are stringent penalties for withdrawing the funds before the specified time.

CD's are safe, and can lock in a better-than-average return for a period of time. They are fully taxable, however. Again, a tax-saving strategy might be to purchase the CD in a child's name.

Compound Interest

How important is a percent or two of interest, anyway? Does it really matter enough to do research and change my savings for the difference between a 6-percent and 8-percent return?

The answer to this question is that a combination of factors determines the significance of interest rates. Not only must the rates be compared, but we must also be concerned with the amount of money to be deposited and the length of time we expect it to remain on deposit.

A $100 deposit left for 1 year at 6-percent interest yields an account balance of $106.

That same $100 left for 1 year at 8-percent interest shows a balance of $108.

But,

A $25,000 deposit left for 1 year at 6 percent has an ending balance of $26,500.

An identical deposit at 8 percent would have an end total
of $27,000 after 1 year—a $500 difference in 12 months.

And,

Two $1000 deposits left for 20 years at 6-percent and 8-per-
cent interest, respectively, would produce accounts of $3207
and $4661, or a difference of over $1400. (Larger than the
original deposit!)

What about regular deposits made over the course of
time? Because compounding means receiving interest on interest, a few percentage points can make a dramatic difference in accumulation.

Consider two families, each trying to save $1000 per year
for 10 years. One will use a 6-percent credit union account,
the other a mutual fund averaging 8 percent per year.

The first family will conclude 10 years having deposited
$10,000 and will find an account balance of $13,972.

The second family will have made the same deposits for the
same length of time, but will see their savings grow to
$15,645. The difference of $1700 represents more than a
year's saved amount over the 10-year time span, for only a
2-percent difference in interest rates.

Can you imagine what an amount of difference would be
made by a 5-percent improvement in interest rates? What
about a 10-percent increase? It's a good thing that compounding makes this degree of difference, because this is precisely
how one can overcome the effects of taxes and inflation. (See
the chart on p. 188.)

Intermediate Term Investments

Somewhat longer than short-term investments, but not
as long as the ten years or greater associated with long-term
investments are the so-called intermediate term programs.
These include savings bonds, treasury notes, and certain conservative balanced-type mutual funds.

U.S. Savings Bonds

U.S. Savings Bonds can be purchased in denominations ranging from as little as $25 to as much as $10,000. They are purchased at about three-quarters of their maturity value and mature in from 5 to 10 years.

Savings bonds now have an interest rate structure in which the earnings vary with market conditions but have a minimum guaranteed rate that increases from the time of purchase to the maturity date.

The yield on savings bonds is taxable, but the income tax due is deferred until the bond is cashed in. Of all the investments we have considered so far, this is the first truly tax-advantaged program and is popular for that reason. Additionally, savings bonds are safe and can often be purchased through a payroll deduction arrangement.

Treasury Notes

Treasury notes are much like treasury bills, except that they have lower minimum purchase amounts (often $5000) and longer maturities (1 to 10 years).

Conservative Mutual Funds

A mutual fund is a pool of investment money invested in accordance with a set of guidelines contained in the mutual fund's prospectus.

Mutual funds are *not* guaranteed, and since their value fluctuates according to market conditions, their value on any given day may be lower than what you paid to acquire them. Some mutual funds have a front-end load, or sales charge, which must be recovered before the investment shows a profit.

Mutual funds allow the purchaser to take his or her share of the dividends earned by the fund in cash, or to have them reinvested in additional shares of the mutual fund.

Mutual funds that invest in stocks or bonds may be conservative, aggressive or very aggressive in intent. The ones that stress maximum preservation of capital while seeking modest growth would be appropriate for intermediate length investments. They often permit as little as $25 monthly contributions, which makes them excellent for small savers.

Mutual fund deposits may have no withdrawal penalty, and can be sold back to the issuing company at any time, and so they are very liquid. Their earnings are subject to taxation, so the chief advantage lies in their ability to diversify a small investment into a proportionate share of a great many companies, and to offer the possibility of a much-above-average return.

Long-Term Investments

Long-term investments are savings programs that should not be undertaken unless the investor is prepared to leave them untouched for 10 years or longer. The need for this length of holding may be caused by contract, specifying a penalty for early withdrawal, or it may be caused by need to average good with bad annual performances.

Generally regarded as long-term investments are treasury bonds, corporate bonds, annuities, life insurance cash values and aggressive mutual funds.

Treasury Bonds

Treasury bonds usually have a $1000-minimum investment. They are safe, and lock in a rate of interest lasting from 10 to 40 years.

Corporate Bonds and Municipal Bonds

Bonds represent the loan of money to a company (corporate) or to a government entity (municipal). Their safety varies with the strength of the issuing institution.

Bonds lock in a rate of return, but may not be suitable investments for all savers, since they trade in $10,000 amounts.

Bonds have some possibility for growth, since a bond that bears a higher interest can be sold for more than the purchase price if interest rates begin to fall. By the same token, they may be worth less than the purchase price if you have to sell prior to maturity and interest rates have risen since the purchase date.

The chief difference between corporate and municipal bonds is that the former are subject to income tax, while the latter are federal income tax exempt. The income tax exemption may extend to state or local income taxes as well.

A *bond fund* is a mutual fund composed of bonds. Like mutual funds that invest in stocks, bond funds may be managed to be either aggressive or conservative in intent. The advantage to the small investor is the ability to participate in the bond market for a lower minimum amount, and to have absolute liquidity. Like other mutual funds, there is no guarantee of performance. There are tax-free bond funds.

A *bond trust* is a fixed collection of bonds designed to be held to maturity. The trust pays interest income to its holders in proportion to their share of ownership. It also can be set up so as to be tax free.

Annuities

Annuities are contracts issued by life insurance companies. They can be purchased with a single deposit, or arranged to accept small deposits over a period of years.

Annuities often have a rear-end load, or surrender charge, which acts as a penalty for early withdrawal. These charges generally decline as the annuity is held until reaching zero after 10 to 15 years.

Modern annuity arrangements offer both a current and a guaranteed minimum rate of interest. When the investor is ready to begin making withdrawal from the annuity, it can be done in a lump sum, but is most often taken in the form of a monthly income payment that is guaranteed to continue for life. The payout may also have both a current and a guaranteed minimum payment amount.

Besides the promise of an income that cannot be "outlived," the greatest plus to annuity contracts is their tax-deferral ability. The earnings accumulating within the annuity are not income-taxable until withdrawn.

Life Insurance Cash Values

The cash-value accumulation in a life insurance policy is also tax deferred. This means that you pay no income tax on the cash values until you begin making withdrawals from the policy, and then, not until the amount you withdraw exceeds the amount of premiums paid.

Some life insurance policies have sales charges that must be recovered before any substantial gain is made. Other policies have surrender charges to discourage early distributions. Either way, life insurance cash values should be regarded as long-term investments.

The combination of being able to accept small contributions, a higher-than-average rate of return, tax deferral and the opportunity to borrow against the funds (and so, have use of them without owing any income taxes) makes life insurance an extremely good choice as a long-term investment.

Aggressive Mutual Funds

Mutual funds that stress growth have the highest potential for returns, far above average. They can accept small contributions, and offer much greater diversity than the ordinary investor would be able to achieve alone.

Because of the risk associated with mutual funds, it is wisest to use them for small, periodic investments, rather than for large, lump-sum amounts. Because mutual funds can have years in which all the trading is at values below what you paid for your shares, it is also wise to allow at least 10 years for the better years to average in with the not-so-good years.

We should not leave the area of mutual fund investments without commenting on a strategy called "dollar cost averaging." This is a systematic investment of identical dollar amounts on a periodic basis (often monthly). Dollar cost averaging actually benefits from a fall in share prices, since the same dollar amount invested would purchase a greater number of shares. When the price per share eventually returns to its original level or higher, the mutual fund owner will discover that he has purchased more shares, and therefore has a higher value to the total investment than if the per share price had gone steadily upward. (See the chart on p. 187.)

> Cal and June Douglas began purchasing mutual funds in the late 1960s at a rate of $25 per month. They continued to do so even when a great many people were scared out of the mutual fund market because the funds had several years of poor performance. Because the Douglases realized they were setting aside money for a long-term investment and the concept of dollar cost averaging was explained to them early on, they realized that even when their mutual fund shares were selling at a lower price, investing the same dollar amount each month allowed them to purchase additional shares.
>
> Over the last 20 years they have seen their mutual funds post some phenomenal gains in a 12-month period, as much as a 50-percent increase in the value per share in 1 year. And they have seen some disastrous years, including one in which the mutual fund shares ended the year selling 15 percent less than what they began. By reinvesting both capital gains and dividends, the Douglases have seen a 20-year average growth of 15 percent per year in their mutual fund holdings. This means that even after having paid taxes each year, their mutual fund investment still tops inflation by some 4 to 5 percent per year.
>
> Now that they are approaching retirement, June and Cal have taken the precaution of converting their more volatile, growth-type mutual fund holdings into a more stable income fund, paying a larger dividend. This amount they will draw off as a monthly retirement supplement, while leaving their principal substantially untouched.

Stocks and Bonds

This book will *not* address the ins-and-outs of selecting individual stocks or bonds. Such an investment should only be undertaken when three criteria have been met:

1. Adequate study has been given to the subject, and to the selected investment.

2. The investor has sought professional advice.

3. The amount invested is that which, if lost, would cause no hardship or change of plans to the investor or his family.

Tangible Investments:
Precious Metals, Collectibles and Real Estate

Tangible property, whether gold and silver, collectibles or land have always been used as hedges against inflation. Since all of these items are purchases of "real" goods, rather than intangible promises to pay, they benefit from inflation and, in fact, increase more rapidly in value in times of higher inflation.

This is not to say that they always show a positive return. Even though you may still own the bar of gold or the piece of fine art, you may receive less than you paid for it at the time liquidation becomes necessary.

Tangible goods have no automatic return; they pay no guaranteed interest. They are subject to loss by theft, fire or other catastrophe and, in the case of property, may be considered "illiquid." In the first place, you must be willing to sell if need be; second, you must locate a buyer who is willing to pay a price you feel is acceptable.

In short, tangible investments have value and can be important additions to a long-term investment portfolio. They should not be entered into lightly, however, or without great study and expert advice.

Investing a Lump-Sum Amount

Lump sums of money may come your way because of the desire to transfer some accumulated savings to a more productive investment vehicle, or by way of an inheritance, or from a particularly large tax refund.

Some advance planning for such an eventuality is wise, because large sums inspire hasty decisions that are perhaps ill-considered, or they cause procrastination, in which the windfall is frittered away.

Some investments lend themselves to lump sums much

better than others. If safety is the paramount concern, banks or credit unions, money market funds or time-saver accounts would be immediately obvious. All of these, together with government obligations, would provide a low to moderate return in safety.

Another consideration in regard to lump-sum investments is whether your objective is immediate income or long-term growth. If the objective is income, purchasing shares of a tax-free bond trust would be appropriate. As discussed before, such an arrangement pays the interest in monthly installments, completely free of federal income tax, and returns the principal at a future (20 to 30 year) date.

If growth is the primary objective for a lump-sum investment, then a mutual fund might be the ideal choice. I recommend the more conservative funds for lump-sum investments, since mutual funds are not guaranteed and there is the risk that the shares could be worth less at the time of liquidation than their purchase cost. It can be historically documented that some very conservative mutual funds have produced 12 to 15 percent annual returns when left undisturbed and when the returns are averaged over 15 to 20 years.

Appropriate Investments by Length of Time
Available for Holding

"Put-and-take"
  Savings account
  Credit union account
  Money market fund
Short term—five years or less
  Certificates of deposit
  Time savings certificates
  Treasury bills
Medium term—five to ten years
  Savings bonds
  Treasury notes
  Conservative mutual funds
Long term—over ten years
  Annuity
  Life insurance cash value
  Treasury bonds
  Aggressive mutual funds
Indeterminate term—redeemed by professional advice
  Stocks
  Bonds

DOLLAR COST AVERAGING

	MUTUAL FUND X		MUTUAL FUND Y	
Invested Amount	Cost per Share	Shares Purchased	Cost per Share	Shares Purchased
$30	$5	6	$5	6
$30	$3	10	$6	5
$30	$1	30	$7	4.3
$30	$1	30	$8	3.75
$30	$3	10	$9	3.33
$30	$5	6	$10	3

Total Invested	Total Shares Owned	Total Shares Owned
$180	92	25.5

TOTAL VALUE AT ENDING PRICE

$$92 \times \$5 = \$460 \qquad 25.5 \times 10 = \$255$$

Even though Fund X performed "miserably," only just regaining its initial share price and Fund Y doubled in per share price for the same period, dollar cost averaging (investing the same amount continuously) clearly favored Fund X.

Compound Interest:
How Much Difference Can Two Percent Make?

Saving $1200 per year for 30 years in a credit union at 6 percent versus saving $100 per month in a mutual fund averaging 8 percent.*

End of Year	6% Investment	8% Investment
1	$ 1,272	$ 1,296
5	7,170	7,603
10	16,766	18,774
15	29,607	35,189
20	46,792	59,308
25	69,787	94,745
30	100,562	146,814

Almost $50,000 difference in the accounts as a result of a 2-percent difference in interest.

*Taxes and inflation *not* considered.

Liquidity Chart

Most Liquid—no penalty or delay
  Savings accounts
  Credit union accounts
  Money market funds
Liquid—some penalty or some delay
  Time saving certificates
  Savings bonds
  Certificates of deposit
  Mutual fund shares
  Life insurance cash values
  Annuity cash values
Least Liquid—perhaps not redeemable at chosen time
  Stocks
  Bonds
  Collectibles
  Real estate
  Tax shelters

Potential Investment Return

Least yield, greatest safety of principal
  Savings accounts
  Credit union accounts
  Money market funds
Low yield, greatest safety of principal
  Savings bonds
  Government obligations
  Certificates of deposit
  Life insurance cash values
  Annuity cash values
Better possible yield, lower safety of principal
  Mutual funds
Best possible yield, least safety of principal
  Stocks
  Bonds

Reviewing My Personal Situation:
Short-Term Savings

1. My emergency fund now contains $_____. This amount equals _____ months income.
2. I am currently putting $_____ into short-term savings. This amount represents _____ percent of my budget.
3. The current interest on my short-term savings is _____ percent.
4. Besides an emergency fund, I have these specific purposes for short-term savings.

   a.

   b.

   c.

Reviewing My Personal Situation:
Long-Term Savings

1. I think the future long-term inflation rate will be: _____ .
2. My tax bracket will probably be 15 percent/28 percent (circle one).
3. I am presently putting $ _____ per month into long-term savings. This amount is _____ percent of my budget.
4. I have _____ years till retirement.
5. My investment philosophy is (circle one).
   a. Absolute safety and a guaranteed return.
   b. A balance of safety and moderate return.
   c. Reasonable safety and above average return.
   d. Superior return, safety a secondary concern.
6. The tax treatment of my long-term savings is (circle one).
   a. No favorable tax treatment.
   b. Tax deferred.
   c. Tax deductible.
   d. Tax free.

13

Retirement Planning

I WANT to remind you of some statistics we reviewed earlier: Out of 100 people who began working at age 25, 16 will have incomes of less than $4000 per year 40 years later, and 52 more will have incomes of less than $25,000 per year.

Does this situation have to exist? If 40 years of working life allows over $1 million to pass through your hands, shouldn't you be able to save some of it for retirement? It seems that there are two reasons why more people are not more successful in their retirement planning. The first, as we said, is the expectation that "someone" else is taking care of it for them and the second is the problem of waiting too long to do something themselves.

Who Else Will Plan Your Retirement?

Many companies provide retirement programs for their employees. If you are eligible for such a plan, can you explain how the program works? Are you contributing to the plan? How much does your employer contribute? Is it a pension or profit-sharing plan? After how many years of employment are you eligible to receive benefits? Is there a sliding scale which provides that your benefit level increases the longer you work? What's the maximum? In what investment are the funds deposited? How secure is it and how profitable? Do you have any say-so in the investment choice?

What options will you have at retirement? If a lump-sum withdrawal is possible, how is it calculated? If you are to receive a monthly benefit, how will it be calculated? Does the plan contain a cost-of-living adjustment? Does the plan provide "joint and survivor" benefits (meaning, will it continue paying your widow or widower if you die first)? How much reduction does the "joint and survivor" option require from what the retirement benefit would be for your lifetime alone?

How much benefit will you receive from Social Security? Is there anything you could be doing to increase that amount? If you want to continue working past age 65, how much can you earn without losing Social Security benefits?

What a ton of questions! Still, whose retirement is it, anyway? Of course I cannot answer all those questions for you. But someone in your company knows the answers! If a company retirement plan exists, then there is a controller, a retirement counselor or a benefits analyst who will go over all this information with you.

My intent in this chapter is to help you organize your questions and to identify areas of particular concern. Even if you belong to a company pension plan, you may discover that you will want to take some additional steps on your own.

What If You're on Your Own?

If your company has no retirement plan, or if you are self-employed, what arrangements have you made to provide retirement income?

If you're depending on Social Security alone, how much benefit will you receive? When will you be eligible to receive it?

Are you eligible for an Individual Retirement Account (IRA)? How much contribution can you make? Where should it be invested for greatest benefit? Are there other retirement plans available for you?

We'll spend some time attempting to answer these questions, because those of you without employment-related retirement plans would like someone to help, wouldn't you?

Key Questions About Retirement Plans

Contributions

One of the first areas of concern you will want to investigate is, how does the money get into the retirement plan? Does the employer contribute an amount equal to a percentage of your salary? How is the percentage determined? If the plan is a profit-sharing program, how is the "profit" amount determined? How is the percentage contributed in your name determined?

Can you make additional contributions to the plan? If you deposit a portion of your salary, does this reduce your taxable income? Will your employer match your contributions? What is the limit of the matching funds?

Vesting

What sort of *vesting* schedule does the plan have? (Vesting means the time of employment required for you to be able to take a portion of the employer's contribution to a retirement plan with you if you leave that company, and what percentage is available to you.)

A typical retirement plan vesting schedule is 100 percent vesting in 5 years—which means you cannot take *any* of the employer's deposits with you until after 5 years of full-time employment, and then you own all of those contributions. Another frequently used program is a schedule in which an employee is 20 percent vested after 3 years employment, 40 percent after 4 years, 60 percent after 5 years, and so on, to 100 percent vested after 7 years.

How do you recover voluntary additional contributions made by you to a retirement plan if you leave before being vested? Can you roll those contributions over into an IRA or another tax-sheltered program?

Investments

Where are the plan funds deposited? Are they in an annuity, mutual funds, stocks or bonds? Who decides how the funds are invested? What has the track record been of investment success?

Can any portion of the deposit be used to purchase life insurance? If so, how much, or what percentage? Can any portion of the deposit be self-directed—meaning, can you have any say-so on how the funds are invested?

Does any portion of the investment have a guarantee? How safe is the principal on deposit? Is there a minimum percentage of interest?

Early Withdrawal

What provisions are there for making a pre-retirement withdrawal? Can you draw on the funds for a financial hardship? What if you became disabled? Would you receive payments only if totally and permanently disabled? What about a temporary or partial disability? How would the payment amount be calculated; for how long would you receive it? If you died after a period of disability, would your family continue receiving payments? For how long? Would the amount change?

What would your family receive if you died while still employed? Would there be a lump-sum option? How would a monthly payment be calculated? How long would it last? Would anything change if you were killed on the job?

How much of your pension would you receive if you retire early? If you were offered any "early out" program, how could you tell if it was a fair offer?

Retirement Income

How much income can you expect monthly at retirement? How is the amount calculated? Is there a maximum percentage you can receive? Is your pension coordinated with Social Security?

If you take an option that continues to pay an income to your family if you died right after retirement, how much lower than a "single life" income would the payments be? Would you be better off to do some pre-retirement investing in a life insurance program, so that you could take a "single life" retirement income and still provide for your spouse?

How much of the pension income is guaranteed? Will it automatically keep up with inflation, or does a group of retirees have to negotiate for increases? Can the pension payment ever be reduced? If so, under what circumstances? Could you take a lump sum?

401(k) Plans

The 401(k) plan, which is named after a section of the Internal Revenue Code, is a substitute for more traditional pension plans and has grown in popularity in the last few years. The majority of employees of large corporations are eligible for 401(k) plans, and a growing number of smaller firms are installing them as well. Companies offering 401(k) plans have found them to be so interesting to their employees that they experience a 75- to 90-percent participation.

The 401(k) plan allows employees to take a portion of their salary and have it payroll deducted, which reduces their taxable income. The amount that can be deducted is sizeable ($7,313 in 1988), greatly exceeding the amount previous programs permitted as deposits. Companies, although not required to do so, may make matching contributions. It is typical, though, for a company to match 50 cents on the dollar up to 4 or 6 percent of the income set aside by the employee. Well over three-fourths of the companies that have 401(k) plans participate in some kind of matching.

The money thus contributed is sheltered from taxation until it is withdrawn. Early withdrawals for "hardship" are permitted, but are subject to a 10-percent penalty, and the amount withdrawn is treated as taxable income. You can see that 401(k) deposits should be thought of as retirement planning. Some 401(k) plans permit the funds to be pledged as collateral for loans, reducing the need for early withdrawals.

The specifics of 401(k) plans vary from company to company. The amount of matching, if any, the terms for withdrawals, the loan possibilities and the allowable contributions are all subject to local modification. Consequently, if your firm has or is considering such a plan, you'll need to get specific information from a company benefit specialist.

The decisions that you as a participant will be called upon to make are:

1. How much to set aside.
2. Where to direct the funds (money market, mutual funds, etc.).
3. When to increase the contributions and by how much.
4. When, if ever, to change the investment vehicle.

What If There Is No Company Pension Plan?

Individual Retirement Accounts

Prior to the 1986 Tax Reform Act, everyone was eligible to contribute to an IRA if they had earned income. A deduction was permitted up to the lesser of the earned income amount or $2000. Non-working spouses were permitted a special "spousal deduction" of $250.

Because the universal application of IRA's has been repealed, many people wrongly believe that they are no longer eligible. Because eligibility is a key issue, we'll deal with it first before examining the rules governing IRA use.

IRA Eligibility

The first rule of eligibility is that if neither you nor your spouse are covered by retirement plans at work, then you are eligible for a fully deductible IRA contribution. Even if your spouse is covered at work, but you are not and you file separate income tax returns, you are still entitled to a fully deductible IRA.

If you are filing a joint return and you are not covered by a retirement plan at work and your spouse is, you may make a fully deductible IRA deposit if your *adjusted gross income* is less than $40,000. Partially deductible IRA contributions can be made for adjusted gross incomes between $40,000 and $50,000. Only if the family joint income exceeds $50,000 (in the situation described) is no deductible IRA deposit allowed.

What if you are covered by a retirement plan at work? Are you ever eligible for a deductible IRA contribution?

Single individuals with work-related retirement programs can have fully deductible IRA's up to $25,000 of adjusted gross income, partially deductible IRA's from $25,000 to $35,000; they are not allowed deductible IRA deposits for over $35,000 of adjusted gross income.

Married individuals with a retirement plan at work who file separate returns are allowed partially deductible IRA deposits up to $10,000 of adjusted gross income.

Why Is Deductibility So Important?

A deduction represents an expense that can be subtracted from your taxable income. Every dollar deducted reduces the amount of income tax you owe by the same percentage as your income tax bracket.

> The Smiths are in the 15-percent federal income tax bracket. A $1000 deduction saves them $150 in taxes ($1000 × 15% = $150).

> The Jones family is in the 28-percent tax bracket. If they contribute $4000 to two IRA's this year, it will save them $1120 in taxes ($4000 × 28% = $1120).

Making a deductible IRA contribution is like having Uncle Sam make part of your retirement savings for you since if you had not made the IRA deposit, you would have had to pay more in taxes than you did.

Individual Retirement Account Provisions

Individual Retirement Accounts allow eligible individuals to make and deduct contributions to retirement programs of their choosing, subject to certain IRS guidelines. Contributions can be made up until April 15 of the year following the calendar year of the tax return.

IRA rules allow up to a $2000 deposit to be deducted per year for workers with at least $2000 of earned income. Intended to be retirement programs, IRA's have a penalty for withdrawals made prior to age 59½. Income must be received from the plan by age 70½, according to a formula determining how much must be withdrawn each yer. The amount withdrawn is then subject to income tax.

During the period of IRA contributions, the interest gained in the IRA is tax deferred. This deferral means that, unlike bank interest or other investment gains which are currently taxed, IRA gains are not taxed until withdrawn.

Because of the tax deduction at the time of contribution and the tax-deferral provision for the gains, IRA's are one of the greatest self-help devices ever permitted by the Internal Revenue Code.

> Denny and Amy Denton are a couple who came to me for counseling regarding their finances, and they expressed a specific interest in retirement planning. Denny was of the opinion that the less involvement with the government program you had the better off you would be in the long run. So, even though Denny had been eligible for an IRA and continues to be eligible under the latest guidelines, he had never taken advantage of the IRA program, preferring instead to invest his $2000 elsewhere.
>
> Denny expressed to me his concern about the money being tied up—that it would be difficult to get to in the event of a pre-retirement need, that the penalties involved for early withdrawal were too drastic to make the program viable and that the government at some future date might "keep all the money." Moreover, he felt that an IRA limited his choice of investments since he believed they had to be arranged through a bank.
>
> I addressed his concerns one at a time but in the reverse order. Individual Retirement Accounts can be arranged with a number of custodial institutions, not just banks. Stock brokerage firms, mutual fund companies, as well as some

other organizations, may have the necessary IRS approval to function as IRA custodians. This means that many investments which look attractive outside of the IRA arrangement can be utilized within the Individual Retirement Account. (This is not true of all investments; for instance, collectibles are no longer allowed to be used in an IRA program.)

It is true that there is a substantial penalty for taking money out of the IRA prior to age 59½. The penalty is 10 percent of the amount withdrawn, or in other words, a $400 penalty on a $4000 withdrawal. A good way to look at this penalty is to consider that if the rate of return the investment has been earning has been at least 10 percent or better, the penalty amounts to the loss of one year's interest on the amount withdrawn. The other "penalty" often referred to is the fact that the amount of money withdrawn prematurely from an IRA is subject to current income tax. But this is actually no more than a balancing of books, since the amount deposited was deductible at the time it was placed in the IRA, and the amount withdrawn will become subject to current taxation anyway, even if that withdrawal is delayed until retirement.

I asked Denny if he would be interested in seeing a comparison of how two similar investments would fare if one were treated as an IRA and the other were not. He and Amy agreed that this would be of interest. I asked him to indicate the amount of deposit planned. He said it was $2000 a year. I allowed him to indicate his tax bracket, which he suggested would be 28 percent. I asked him to pick an interest rate that he felt would be reasonable over a long-term period of time. He mentioned that since he was pretty conservative in his investment philosophy, he would be satisfied with the long-term gain of only 8 percent per year.

The $2000 annual deposit at an assumed rate of 8 percent a year would amount to a shade under $28,000 after 10 years in a non-IRA deposit. The same deposit made into an IRA for the same 10-year period would produce over $31,000. Because compound interest produces ever more dramatic results over longer periods of time, a similar comparison at the end of 20 years shows the non-IRA investment having about a $74,000 value, while the IRA account shows almost $100,000 in value.

When we worked the projection out to Denny's retirement

at 65, the difference favored the IRA account by almost $100,000. The IRA investment amounted to a total of $244,000, while the same investment in a fully taxable account amounted to only $155,000. In addition, I pointed out to Denny that each year's $2000 deposit saved his family about $560 annually in taxes, based on his estimate of a 28-percent bracket.

Amy wanted to know if the return that they could expect in the IRA account would be as good as that in the non-IRA. My answer is, the return should be identical for identical investments. Or, by way of an example, many insurance companies issue annuity contracts that can be purchased either in IRA or non-IRA form. The declared interest rate on those is currently around 8 percent, and that amount of interest credited would be the same whether the investment was made in IRA form or not. What this means is that on even higher rates of return, the IRA investment is favored even more decisively; for instance, a 12-percent projection, as would be the case in some mutual funds, would show not double but triple the difference in favor of the IRA after a 30-year investment period.

What Denny and Amy have elected to do after reexamining their investment philosophy is to divide their savings program between an IRA and a non-tax-qualified plan—leaving the one strictly as a retirement program and having full access to the other without the penalty (Denny's biggest, original concern).

What About Nondeductible IRAs?

While the deductibility of IRA contributions is clearly their chief advantage, those tax payers who are not eligible for an IRA deduction should still consider IRA deposits.

The reason that many wage earners who are looking toward retirement will wish to make IRA contributions (even if they have a retirement plan at work) is simple. If you are trying to build a retirement supplement, it needs to be stored in a tax-deferred location or its effectiveness will be reduced.

Consider two annual deposits of $2000. Both are made into programs paying 8-percent interest.

Both families are in the 28-percent tax bracket. One family saves the money in a nondeductible IRA (still tax-deferred), while the other family invests in a program without tax benefit.

After 10 years, the family using the IRA has an account balance of $31,290, while the second family's balance shows a figure of about $27,500.

After 25 years, at a time when each family has set aside $50,000, the family with the IRA has $157,000, while the other family has only $112,000.

Doubling your money is pretty good planning—but wouldn't *tripling* be even better?

What Are Suitable Individual Retirement Account Investments?

Many banks, savings and loans, and credit unions offer IRA's in the form of certificates of deposit and other time deposit accounts. They also allow the funds to be rolled over to continue the IRA deposit without incurring taxes when the time period elapses. Such an investment would be extremely safe, but would suffer the fate of all guaranteed savings when thrust up against the effects of inflation.

Because IRA's are intended to be retirement savings, you should apply the same kind of reasoning regarding appropriate deposits as was discussed in the section on long-term investing. If you have longer than 10 years till retirement, you should consider a mutual fund with an opportunity for capital growth.

If you have fewer than 10 years to retirement, or if your investment philosophy requires an even smaller degree of risk, then a conservative "capital preservation" fund may be for you.

Still more conservative would be a plan in which your IRA's are invested in annuity contracts.

It is not required that your IRA's be all in the same investment, or even that it always be made with the same firm. In fact, prudence would dictate that you examine the possibilities each year and make your careful selection. As you near retirement, don't hesitate to move the funds to new or more suitable investments. On the other hand, don't move just for "newness'" sake. Remember, mutual funds in particular require the time to really demonstrate their performance. A fund that has one "down" year may be the fund with the best 10- or 20-year average.

Concluding Thoughts

Retirement planning is only difficult in that it requires your current attention to what appears to be a future problem. The justification for working now on a 20- or 30-year distant circumstance is that failing to do so may condemn you to years of struggling to make ends meet instead of pleasant relaxation. As life expectancy continues to increase, the number of individuals who will find that they have outlived their retirement income will continue to rise. I assume that you don't want to be one of them.

If you presently have a retirement plan, get familiar with it. Study carefully any proposed changes. If you are contemplating a new career or company, be sure to enter the differences in pensions into your calculations.

If you don't have a present retirement plan, start one. Even a modest savings now, dedicated strictly to retirement, will pay large dividends later. Remember, only $25 a month set aside amounts to over $50,000 in 30 years. Treat yourself to all the tax advantages to which you're entitled, and seek professional advice if you're uncertain as to what investment would be best for you.

Planning for Retirement

Of 100 Workers Employed at Age 25*
  By Age 65:

      29 have died
      16 have annual incomes under $4000

---

*U.S. Dept. Health and Human Services, 1983.

52 have annual incomes between $4000 and $25,000
3 have annual incomes over $25,000

Reviewing My Personal Situation:
Retirement Planning

1. I do/don't have a retirement plan at work.
   a. I will be fully vested in _____ years.
   b. The plan currently invests in _____ .
   c. I have/don't have a choice of investments.
   d. I can/can't make emergency withdrawals.
   e. My projected monthly retirement income is
      _____ for a "joint-and-survivor" plan.
      _____ for a "single life only" plan.
2. My company does/does not have a plan to which I can make voluntary contributions.
   a. My company will/won't match my contributions.
   b. I have a choice of _____ different investments.
      These are_____.
3. I am/am not eligible for a deductible IRA.
   a. My attitude toward retirement investments is conservative/moderate/aggressive.
   b. Therefore, an appropriate IRA choice for me would be
      _____.

Appendix A
Social Security

OVER TWO-THIRDS of the workers who worked for 40 years to retirement are relying on the Social Security system to provide from 50 to 100 percent of their retirement income. What is this government entity, really? How did it start, and what does it do?

The Structure of Social Security

The Social Security system came about as a result of the economic upheaval of the Great Depression. The Social Security Act was passed in 1935, and is most often thought of as dealing with the three areas of retirement, disability and survivor benefits. The act also provided for several state-administered programs, including unemployment compensation, old-age assistance and aid to the disabled.

Funding for Social Security

The Social Security program is funded by a tax on each eligible employee, which is shared half-and-half by the employer and the employee. Some professions with their own retirement programs, such as public-school teachers, are exempt from participation in Social Security. Self-employed individuals must pay both portions of the tax, which now amounts to approximately 15 percent of income.

Since the tax contributions of current workers are used in part to pay the benefits to retired workers, and since the benefit level increases to keep pace with inflation, it follows that the tax levied must increase as more of our population reaches older ages and becomes eligible to receive payments.

The tax rate is applied to a maximum income amount, but as this amount is increased each year and already exceeds $40,000, the vast majority of workers pay social security taxes on their entire wages.

Survivor Benefits

There is a $255 lump-sum death benefit paid when a worker dies; this has never been changed since the program began. More importantly, there are survivor benefits paid to a widow with dependent children or to the children themselves.

The amount varies with the worker's age and average income, and is subject to a family maximum benefit amount. The current family maximum is about $1800 of monthly income. Since this figure depends on an annual earnings base of $45,000, the average amount actually paid out is probably closer to $1400 per month.

The most notorious feature of the survivor benefits program has to do with the fact that once the last dependent child reaches the age of 18, a surviving spouse is no longer eligible for *any* survivor payments until he or she reaches the age of 60 (except in cases involving disability). This so-called "black-out" period is one of the most overlooked gaps in any family's financial security planning.

Retirement Benefits

The second category of Social Security benefits is that of old-age assistance. Eligibility for retirement income payments depends on being "fully insured." What this means is that a worker must have participated in the Social Security program for 40 calendar quarters.

Assuming that this requirement has been met, the amount of monthly income available at age 65 depends on the average earnings. There is a reduced benefit amount available as early as age 62, but it is only 80 percent of what would have been received at age 65. Other information regarding payments:

1. While the wife of a retired worker is eligible either for benefits based on her husband's record of earnings or on her own wage record, she may not receive both.

2. Retired workers receiving Social Security retirement benefits are limited in the amount of employment compensation they can be paid without a loss of payment.

A worker can obtain information about quarters of qualification and earnings status by writing to:

> Social Security Administration
> P.O. Box 20
> Wilkes-Barre, PA 18703

Be sure to give your full name, date of birth and Social Security number when writing for information.

Disability Income

The final area of Social Security benefits is disability income assistance. If an employee is fully insured by the definition of the Social Security system, and is disabled to the extent of being unable to perform any financially gainful work by a disability expected to last at least 12 months, then the worker is entitled to receive a monthly disability payment.

Again, the income amount is determined by age and earnings and is subject to a family maximum amount. As we have discussed elsewhere, it is extremely difficult to qualify for Social Security disability benefits, and there is a 5-month waiting period for which no benefits are paid.

Appendix B
Choosing Advisors

IN THE COURSE of one week's perusal of a newspaper, it is possible to find the following: financial planning seminars offered by a man who counsels investment in real estate; informational meetings with the local office of a national stock brokerage firm; workshops with a traveling lecturer who advises the purchase of gold as a hedge against inflation; and an advertisement by a well-known insurance company that states: "Single-premium life insurance is the answer to your financial planning needs."

Where is one to turn for advice? Since there are tax matters and legal concerns and investment questions that are too complex and too time consuming for the average investor to single-handedly cope with, how can one obtain expert assistance?

Many people find they have acquired advisors almost by default. It is not uncommon for families to have a tax preparer who makes tax-planning suggestions, an attorney who has assisted in some legal entanglement; and very likely several insurance agents. Although surveys report that most people would prefer to have all their insurance with one agent, many families have three or more insurance agents handling different policies. Are there some guidelines for selecting advisors? We can identify three.

Principles to Follow in Selecting Advisors

The first point to remember in choosing an advisor is to visit with friends and relatives whose opinions you value. Find out what advisors they have for needs similar to yours. Discuss with them how satisfied they are with the service they have received, how available the advisor is when needed, and how conscientious he is about offering advice.

The two most frequent complaints heard about advisors who are *not* recommended are: "I can't reach him when I need him," and "He doesn't show attention to my concerns." Someone who is able to satisfy your friends with similar concerns has a greater likelihood of helping you also.

This kind of word-of-mouth referral will assist you in locating an advisor suitable for your needs. (For instance, a CPA who does corporate returns for a living may have greater visibility in your community, but might not be as helpful to you as a less well-known family practitioner.)

The second principle is to examine the list to identify those Christian brothers and sisters in the professional roles needed.

I make this point, not out of chauvinism, but rather out of a closely held belief that it's important to have an advisor with whom you can pray over a thorny decision. You want someone who can be counted on to give the Lord first place in his or her business, just as you do in your own.

(I should say that I have listed principles one and two in the order given because I do not find Christianity to be any substitute for professional competence, nor any guarantee of business satisfaction.)

The final point in regard to selecting an advisor has to do with that individual's professionalism and ongoing training.

Does the advisor you are considering belong to the appropriate professional organizations? Does he or she participate in the local accounting organization, Bar association, or life underwriters association? What advanced degrees or designations has the advisor sought? Is there evidence of current participation in workshops and training seminars, so that the level of expertise remains top-notch?

Incidentally, it should not be offensive to any of the professionals from whom you are seeking advice for you to inquire into background, training and present studies. Attorneys, accountants and agents exist by providing *service*; they need to go out of their way to make the client comfortable and satisfied. Anyone who would take offense at a respectful scrutiny does not deserve your business. I want my financial affairs handled with an attitude of concern and caring.

Fifteen years ago I could still do a great many of my own car repairs, but today I am not "up" on fuel-injected, front-wheel drive, computer-adjusted, electronic ignition vehicles. I not only expect a competent professional to handle this for me, I want that individual to stay current as well.

Professional Designations to Look For

In the realm of insurance, look for evidence of professionalism by the following designations:

Registered Representative—Required for mutual funds sales.
LUTCF—Fellow of the Life Underwriter's Training Council
CLU—Chartered Life Underwriter
ChFC—Chartered Financial Consultant
CPCU—Chartered Property and Casualty Underwriter
RHU—Registered Health Underwriter
CFP—Certified Financial Planner

The last designation listed, CFP, is sought by professionals other than insurance agents and is coming to be recognized as a standard of competence for those offering investment advice.

Bookkeepers and accountants who practice tax preparation and planning should have the designation "Enrolled Agent," meaning they are familiar with current tax laws. The title CPA, or Certified Public Accountant, also represents many hours of study, experience and ongoing training.

Attorneys may not necessarily have additional designations, but you will want to explore the type of practice they have. They may also seek designation as "Enrolled Agents" or "CFP's."

A Warning About "Financial Planners"

A great many individuals style themselves as "financial planners." You should know that this is a much-abused title, which may not have any substance.

Investment advisors are supposed to be registered with the Securities and Exchange Commission, and there is an earned designation of Certified Financial Planner, but both can be claimed fraudulently and neither is a guarantee of legitimacy.

Newsweek reported in its August 29, 1988, issue that some 22,000 investors have lost $400 million to financial planning fraud in just a 2-year period. Sadly, many of these were people who were trying to get the most mileage out of their retirement nest egg, only to find themselves bilked out of all their savings.

A valuable resource to aid you in understanding (and avoiding) investment fraud is the book entitled *Investor Alert!* It is sponsored jointly by the North American Securities Administrators Association and the Council of Better Business Bureaus, and should be available by contacting those organizations.

It suggests 10 dos and don'ts for investors, which I believe are important to review:

1. Be wary of unexpected calls or letters offering quick profits but requiring immediate investment.

2. Be skeptical of promises to double your investment or pay high returns in a short time.

3. Turn down investment requests accompanied by high-pressure tactics like "tomorrow will be too late."

4. Always demand written records of past performance, but be aware that these can be faked.

5. Be suspicious of advice offered as "inside information" or "hot tips."

6. Ask for a prospectus or offering circular and read it carefully before investing.

7. Seek professional advice from your accountant, attorney or other reliable consultant.

8. Deal whenever possible with established, reputable, local firms. If this is not possible, consult your Better Business Bureau or the appropriate regulatory agency.

9. If hounded by a phone solicitation or promotion, hang up.

10. When in doubt, *don't!*

Concluding Thoughts

Work out your own family's needs and goals before seeking advice. Be able to set forth clearly a statement of your intent, then allow the professional to make suggestions as to how to achieve your desires.

The one situation in which you absolutely must have assistance is tax return preparation. You and I just cannot be as well-versed on the current tax law changes as a competent professional; we would almost certainly overlook deductions to which we are entitled.

Reviewing My Personal Situation:
Choosing Advisors

1. I presently have (circle which apply):
   a. Accountant/CPA
   b. Attorney
   c. Tax-preparer
   d. Insurance Agent

2. Of the above advisors (circle which applies):
   a. I am happy with all of them and seek their advice.
   b. I am happy with some of them.
   c. I am unsure about seeking their advice.
3. Of the above advisors (circle which apply):
   a. I know about their background and training.
   b. I know about their present professional standing.
   c. I know about their spiritual condition.
   d. I can compare notes with friends whose opinions I value about their experiences with these advisors.

Appendix C
The Importance of a Will

ANY DISCUSSION of wills is bound to be upsetting. First, wills make us unhappy by forcing us to contemplate the mortality of our loved ones and ourselves. Second, out of the general population, only one out of three couples have done the necessary preparation to avoid lengthy and costly probate, and therefore find the entire will-writing process still ahead of them. Third, wills upset us when we find out that we can't just do it once and forget it; they are living entities that need to respond to changes in our circumstances.

While most people believe that property is difficult to acquire, they naively expect that its distribution will be a simple matter. The unpleasantness of the subject results in putting off doing anything about it, often leaving families in the lurch and creating unnecessary delays in settlement and avoidable expenses.

The Individual Without a Will

If an individual dies, property may pass into the temporary control of a probate court until transferred to the new rightful owner. This transfer process, which could involve as little as one savings account, may result in disagreements among survivors, the surfacing of unsuspected or forgotten debts, or other claims against the estate.

Have you heard the expression, "If you die without a will, the state will write one for you?" It's true. This means that in the absence of a will (intestate), the state will determine the appropriate distribution of property, even if such dispersal was contrary to what the deceased might have wished.

Furthermore, in the absence of an executor (named in a will), the court will appoint an administrator, who might not have been the first choice of the deceased and might not act according to the desires the deceased would have expressed. Even such a fundamental question as naming a guardian for minor children will be decided by the courts in the absence of a will.

The Need for Professional Assistance

You may have heard that handwritten and videotaped wills have been judged valid. Some people see this as a chance to save on attorney fees. What false economy! Even if there are examples where such a "do-it-yourself" approach has worked, you need to know that even a small technicality, like knowing the correct number of witnesses required by your state, can invalidate your best efforts.

I'm not going to attempt to give any specific advice about drawing up a will in this section—first, because I'm not a legal professional; second, because I don't want you to try to write your own; and third, because laws about wills vary from state to state.

When Do You Need a Will?

What about a young couple with no children and no appreciable property as yet? It is better to sit down now with appropriate legal counsel and raise the pertinent issues so as to establish a framework for future decisions than to gamble on picking the "right moment." Do you believe that you could judge when the amount of your belongings reach the size to be "important enough" to draw up a will?

What About Updating?

Review your will with legal assistance whenever a major change occurs, such as opening a business of your own, purchasing a new piece of property, having a new baby, or seeing one of your children pass the age of eighteen.

Also, keep track of details internal to the will, such as if the person you had selected as executor has died, or if the family named as guardian to your children should move out of your area.

In any case, go over your will at least every 3 years, even if you believe that nothing major has changed.

> The Silvers visited an attorney with the view of having a will drawn up. Even though they took home a preliminary fact-finding questionnaire, they kept putting off completing it. Perhaps they didn't want to come up with the $200 fee, who knows?
>
> About a year later, Mr. Silver died suddenly of a heart attack. The probate court held that the widow had to report back each year to give an accounting of how the money was spent in caring for the children, and required that she post a performance bond to guarantee that she used proper judgment in spending the children's money. You see, she was the children's stepmother, and the will had not been changed since Mr. Silver had remarried!
>
> This business of reopening the estate each year cost several thousand dollars in fees over 4 years—many times over the original amount it would have required to have the will redrawn properly.

Reviewing My Personal Situation:

Wills

1. I have/don't have a will prepared by an attorney.
2. My will was updated on _____ (date).
3. My will appoints _____ as executor.
4. My will names _____ as guardian of my children.
5. My spouse knows/does not know the location of my will and its provisions.

A Christian Financial Creed

Inasmuch as God has entrusted me with certain material possessions, and inasmuch as I acknowledge His ownership and my stewardship, and inasmuch as He has expectations regarding my management of those possessions, I therefore pledge to . . .

• SEEK His will in regard to income, expenses, tithing, debt, taxes, insurance and investments;

• ADOPT the lessons of Scripture regarding proper attitudes toward money and possessions;

• BECOME knowledgeable about financial management so as to enjoy His approval;

• CONSIDER prayerfully my household budget, my offerings and my obligations so as to be reckoned a faithful witness;

• DEVELOP investments wisely and carefully so as to make the best use of His abundance for my family and for others;

• ENACT prudent preparations against financial misfortune;

• FIND His will in regard to income, expenses, tithing, debt, taxes, insurance, and investments and

• GRASP entirely His promise recorded in Prov. 3:6: "In all your ways acknowledge him, and he will make your paths straight."